Mica!
Brusseau

Capel
Wetmell

Lexi
waters

Let There Be Light

PLEASE!

A
SIGN LANGUAGE
INTERPRETER
VIEWS YOUR CLASS
FROM BEHIND HIS HANDS

Jim Brewington

Copyright © 2002 by H. James Brewington

ISBN 0-7414-1424-4

Published by:

PUBLISHING.COM

519 West Lancaster Avenue
Haverford, PA 19041-1413
Info@buybooksontheweb.com
www.buybooksontheweb.com
Toll-free (877) BUY BOOK
Local Phone (610) 520-2500
Fax (610) 519-0261

Printed in the United States of America

Printed on Recycled Paper

Published February 2003

Appreciation

I have received encouragement and many helpful
suggestions from faculty members and Special
Services professionals at Saddleback College including Cheryl Altman, Ginny Harris, Loma
Hopkins, Carolyn Kuykendall, and Will Summers.
To them all, whom I consider my valued friends,
goes my admiration and gratitude.

The efforts of many skilled people have converged
over the years to provide for my learning American
Sign Language. Included are deaf students, other
interpreters, friends from the deaf community, and
the following professors of ASL who have taught me
well at Saddleback College:

David Chapman, Julie Chapman, Scott Kramer,
Adrianne Kosek, Etta Stecker, Rusty Stecker, and
David Thompson.

I applaud you and your work. I think of you often
with fondness.

Cover Design

Thank you to Amy Jones for her photography and to
John W. Freyer and Mary O'Malley whose creative
brilliance added much light to this work.

Table of Contents

"To be proud of knowledge is to be blind with light."

—Benjamin Franklin

PREFACE

Who was it who told me years ago that most book readers don't read prefaces? Someone, somewhere in academia, back in my university days, I think. How was this skip-the-preface hypotheses proven? Did someone actually empirically research it? Was there a federal grant?

I don't know, but the concept became indelible in my brain. I've read every preface I've encountered since, sometimes with benefit.

Because you, my fellow preface-reader, are plunged in, you deserve an award or two, something helpful the others will miss.

AWARD #1

Point 1—A word about a culture: The deaf are the only people with a shared physiological abnormality who have their own culture. I believe this is because the deaf are the only such people who have their own language, and language is one of the basic components of culture.

The deaf culture is a subculture in our society, a subculture with its own language, traditions, social values, etiquette, jokes and humor, and view of life. Not all people who are deaf choose to associate closely with the deaf culture, but many do. Often in writings and literature regarding deaf people, those who partake of deaf culture are referred to as "the Deaf" with a capital *D*. Deaf people who live outside of the deaf culture are referred to as "the deaf" —lowercase *d*. Hence some people who are deaf are not Deaf. The uppercase-lowercase distinction is useful in many contexts. I have, however, chosen not to use the capitalization method for differentiating the two groups of deaf persons for a couple of reasons:

First, while no attitudes of superiority or inferiority may exist in the hearts of the two deaf groups, an implication of such feelings seems to ooze and trickle forth from those who press the contrast.

Second, the existence of the deaf's subculture is assured and vividly clear to those in it or near it. Contrastingly, knowledge of the subculture and its characterizations is esoteric. Consequently, subtle written distinctions (*D*'s and *d*'s) may cause ambiguity and confusion instead of clarity in the minds of hearing people, especially that supposed vast majority who don't read prefaces.

To my good friends in the deaf community, please know that I do not in anyway de-emphasize the charm, warmth, richness, and value of your culture. Thank you for understanding the leeway I've taken in choosing not to hold fast to the *D-d* tradition

Point 2—A word about a word or two: Some of my deaf friends are offended if they are described as *disabled*. I find little or no significant meaning or application difference between *disabled* and *impaired*. Being described as hearing *impaired* is acceptable to every deaf person I've known; being described as hearing *disabled* is offensive to some. Yet I sometimes use *disabled* in this text. I do not want to offend my current or future friends. I do not want to be controlled by their various word preferences either. Being forced to tiptoe through the politically correct tulips when there are no lexicological weeds is a hike too delicate for my tastes. Words whose denotations and connotations convey the wrong idea should be avoided, of course. But any group that declares particular words offensive for no discernable lexicological reason and then thrusts that value on all people is a group that widens the gap between people instead of bridging it. I find *disabled* neither derogatory nor offensive, and I tend, therefore, to use it interchangeably with *impaired*.

The word *handicapped* is a different story though. Although *handicapped* is used extensively in everyday speech, on public access signs, on special parking placards, and so forth, the trend now is to use the preferred expressions *disabled* or *people with disabilities*. The label *handicapped* seems to insinuate the designated person cannot accomplish on even terms with most other people. The term *disabled* hints the person can achieve equally if accommodations are made or if things may be done in a different way. So, technically, a *disabled* person confined to a wheelchair is hindered and therefore *handicapped* if ramps are not available and is not *handicapped* if ramps are present. For many people *handicapped* carries a negative connotation because of the erroneous belief that the word is derived from the image of a street beggar. Actually *handicapped* comes from the phrase *hand in cap*, originally a game of chance in which forfeits were drawn from a cap.

These distinctions, while engaging, may or may not be important. Correct word choice to convey correct meaning is truly valuable. Word choice that is demanded for the emotional or political benefit of a few people adds unnecessary complexity to human relationships.

AWARD #2

Let There Be Light PLEASE! is not a research project in the usual sense. This work is not a book about the deaf written by a hearing person for other hearing people. It is a book written by an interpreter about interpreting. It is for people who use the services of an interpreter or anyone else interested or curious. It is an expression of my experiences, my observations, my opinions, and my conclusions from the perspective of a sign language interpreter. Even the definitions in the glossary are my thoughts and words laced, in some cases, with my opinions and perhaps with my biases, which definitions are constructed from my studies and training and background connected with interpreting. (*The Registry of Interpreters for the Deaf, Inc., (RID) "Code of Ethics" reproduced in Chapter 8 is an exception. It is reproduced verbatim.*) Interpreters stand between two worlds, the hearing world and the deaf world. We are granted glimpses of both worlds. If you would like to see what I've been shown, examine what

I've concluded, and read what I feel, you are invited to proceed.

Because this writing is not a traditional research work, you'll find no notes or references in the back. I've refused to use those distracting, annoying small-print footnotes at the bottoms of pages that demand the reader's eyes fly up and down performing touch-and-go's between fact and anecdote.

The masculine pronoun has been used throughout the book to avoid the awkward he/she, him/her, himself/herself constructions.

Finally, notification of any mistakes I may have made or of any disagreements you may have will be welcomed by me personally. Let's do lunch!

"*Lead, Kindly Light, amid*
the encircling gloom,
Lead Thou me on!
The night is dark, and I am
far from home
Lead Thou me on!

—John Henry Newman

v

"Light; or, failing that, lightning: the world can take its choice."

—Thomas Carlyle

Introduction

Do you hear well? If the answer is yes, as a person with normal hearing, chances are good you would avoid a deaf person if one were nearby you. Oftentimes, deaf people avoid the hearing. The primary reason is that neither group has the facility to talk easily and clearly with the other. Between the deaf and the hearing is a gorge of silence, wide and deep. In the dark vastness of this bottomless abyss is lost one of the tools of understanding and friendship: language. At best, discourse between the deaf and the hearing is awkward and faulty; at worst, it is impossible. The silence does not exist only in the ears of the deaf, but also on the lips of the hearing who muzzle themselves and shy from those who cannot hear. The resulting hush is not peaceful and calm and restful. On the contrary, the quiet becomes an agitated and unsettled separation devoid of the richness of relationship, a separation shored apart by a wedge of misunderstanding. Such need not be! I hope this writing will help to eliminate some of the controlling ignorance and provide some of the needed information to bridge the chasm between the hearing and the deaf.

One structural component of the bridge that spans the gulf of quiet, twixt deaf and hearing, is a strange character hanging in suspense: **The Interpreter**.

If you are hearing impaired and sign language is your primary language, interpreters are probably commonplace and routine in your life. If you are hearing and the only signs you know are the ones you use in traffic jams, chances are you have never even met an interpreter, let alone worked with one. Besides, signs used in traffic jams don't need an interpreter!

I am an interpreter. I work mostly, but not exclusively, in college classrooms where the instructor is hearing and one or more of the students are deaf. Just before the beginning of each semester I try to meet with the instructors of my assigned classes. Now I'm a fairly confident guy usually, a teacher myself with years of public speaking under my belt, but I want to tell you that meeting the instructors for the first time to inform them that I will be in their classroom all semester is awkward. I am usually tinged with a small dose of trepidation, believing I am walking into a semi-hostile environment darkened by misunderstanding about my role and my relationship with the teacher, the deaf student, and the hearing students. As an interpreter in the classroom, just like a good, taxpaying citizen at the DMV or a student at the Admissions and Records Office, I have every right to be in the classroom. I'm even supposed to be there. During these introductory meetings, some of the instructors I encounter are unfriendly to borderline cordial, and somehow I know from the get-go that this time together, initiated by me, will be terminated by them, and, in the end, I will not be completely heard or understood.

So, in an attempt to alleviate awkwardness; to promote efficient and enjoyable partnerships of teachers, interpreters, and students; to inform; to dare to advise; and perchance to entertain—oh yes, and to get this stuff off my chest—I have written this primer.

It's a book for the teachers at Saddleback College, where I am privileged to work, or teachers at any other school; it's a book for students, hearing or deaf; it's a book for interpreters who serve the hearing and the deaf; it's a book for anyone who would like a tighter grip on the blessings available through understanding what the other person has to say.

Important for all to know: I do not pretend or portend to be an expert at anything. While I mention deaf culture, I am not a member of that culture, though I am graciously invited to visit there from time to time. I do not present myself as a representative of deaf people, although I do not hesitate to relay to you some of the thoughts and opinions that certain deaf individuals have related to me. I have never been deaf, even for a moment, even when I have tried unsuccessfully to block sound with ear plugs. I have forced myself to watch television without the volume, but I can always hear anytime I want. Consequently, I cannot write about deaf life from experience. All of my experiences are from the hearing side of silence.

Though I have spent more than the average number of years attending colleges and universities as a student, and as an interpreter, and though I have been a teacher of adults for many years, I have never been employed as a college teacher. I don't pretend to be a skilled college educator. I took six units of education courses at Texas Tech University in the early 1960's. That hardly qualifies me to give teachers advice about how to teach. I admit I do have quiet thoughts during the teaching process about which techniques seem effective on the one hand, and which seem insensitive to the students' needs and ineffective on the other. Some of those heretofore private musings about teachers, students, subjects, and myself are written into the main body of this work. They, and other elaborations, are enclosed in parenthesis and printed in bold italics.

Both the hearing and the deaf who know me will, I think, acknowledge that I know a little bit about how to communicate with each group. *Voici!* My only credential for being so bold as to ask you to read on. Because I do communicate with members of both groups almost everyday and because I assist people in both groups in their communication with each other, I have insights and frustrations unique to interpreters, and I have emotionally touching and amusing experiences unique to me. Why shouldn't you join with me in the insights and the blasted frustrations? Perhaps you will discover something emotionally touching in these pages, and maybe you will even have a smile or two — or more.

"More Light!"

—Johann Wolfgang von Goethe's last words

"We must be as courteous to a man as we are to a picture, which we are willing to give the advantage of a good light."

—Ralph Waldo Emerson

CHAPTER 1

The Beginning of Our Understanding

(A Necessary Overview)

If you can, try to imagine for a moment that you can't hear anything and that you never have heard anything. You are profoundly deaf and have been since your birth. You have never heard your mom's voice or your dad's voice. You have never heard the sound of rain in the autumn of the year or the crunch of snow packing under your walking feet in the winter. You have never heard the birds chirping in the spring or the surf's breaking or the crackling of fire in a fire pit at the beach in the summer.

You have never experienced the excitement or soothing calm brought on by music, for you have never heard music or a radio or a television or a movie. You have never heard anyone read you a story or tell you a

1

joke. You have never heard laughter or sobbing—or the screams of friends on a roller coaster. You've never even heard the roller coaster.

You don't hear the host calling your name at a restaurant. You've never talked on the phone. When you're at the airport, the security guards don't consider that you didn't hear the alarm sound as you passed through the metal detector. No one knows you didn't hear which gate is yours. On the plane, you don't receive the baggage claim information or the connecting gate number from the flight attendant's announcement. In your hotel room, you can't order from room service or call for your messages from the front desk or have a wake-up call or know that your friend is knocking at the door or that the fire alarm is blaring.

You try to speak the English language, but you have never heard English (*or any other language*) spoken. And anyway English is, at best, a second language for you—second after American Sign Language (*ASL*) and maybe third after an educational sign language you learned in school before you learned ASL. You've never heard the sound of your own voice. You don't form sounds correctly. Most hearing people disregard your speech—and you. Many conclude that you are mentally retarded and treat you so, even though your mind is sharp. You are perhaps formally educated and your sensory perceptions, other than hearing, are phenomenally sharp and astute. The extent of what you can see in your peripheral vision is astounding, and your ability to see background, its scope and detail, while focusing on foreground—perhaps understanding two sign language conversations at once—is unbelievable to a hearing person.

Also, you've experienced ignorance and the desire for an education. You sense strongly the importance of knowing what educated people know. But you've never heard anyone read a book to you. You've never heard a lecture or a teaching tape. You've never heard students kick around a topic in a discussion group. You've never heard anyone ask a question in class, and you've never heard anyone answer one. You've never heard anyone "amen" or "right-on" a point that touched the heart during a teaching.

You have never had a conversation with a teacher. No teacher knows your language, so you can't counsel with one or have a private talk with one unless you use an interpreter—who may be a stranger to you.

Perhaps you have attended a college that provides "Special Services." That means you sit in the front row in class where the deaf must sit. You face an interpreter who converts speech and other sounds to hand movements and facial expressions by means of a beautiful, but conspicuous, sign language. Then a hearing teacher instructs hearing students in a "foreign" language (*English*). The teacher illustrates his lecture with examples from television news reports and other sources from the hearing world. He tells jokes using English puns and other plays on English words, and he flowers his talk with English idioms and figures of speech that do not translate clearly into your language. Because schools usually budget little for interpreter services, your interpreter may be inexpert or even inept and maladroit. There are no textbooks printed in American Sign, your native language.

Typically, the hearing teachers and students receive no information or education about the deaf person's language, culture, or life style. They have never heard of a deaf culture. For the most part they do not know how to communicate with you even through an interpreter. And while their desire is to include you, they don't know how. Many of them live with the myth that all deaf people read lips and that lipreading bridges the communication gap completely. In an effort to help, they overmouth words, exaggerate facial expressions, and yell.

Your justified and understandable conclusion is that college is not pleasant; it's an apprehensive and frustrating ordeal.

You experience and deal with all the usual human feelings of any other person—desire for love and acceptance, friendship, positive recognition, affirmation, and independence. You know loneliness, fear, rejection, pain, failure, and depression. You are familiar with joy, silliness, funny sarcasm, victory in sports and business. In relationships you've experienced separation and reconciliation, and of course you love life.

Now imagine that you are not deaf but rather hard of hearing. For the hearing world that means you *can not* hear some things. For the deaf world that means you *can* hear some things. While you are not black-balled by either community, you are not fully accepted and included in either one. If you sign at all, your skills are perhaps not fluent, and many deaf, for cultural reasons, do not fully accept you. The hearing world falsely believes that the hearing aids they see you wear are bringing you up-to-speed, that you hear fine, and yet most of the time you miss most of what is being said, and at no time do you hear all of what's going on.

Well, this trip in our imagination, the imagination of the hearing, extends far beyond my ability to write about it and yours to comprehend it. We who hear cannot understand what happens on the other side of the wall of deafness, in the hush of muffled quiet. Many of the deaf have never been, or cannot remember being, on the hearing side of this wall that all too often separates those of us who hear well from those of us who don't.

All people, hearing or hearing impaired, understand the feeling of being shunned and ignored, out of the loop, or downright excluded. The feeling is awful. The opposing feeling of being embraced, accepted, and included has no emotional equal. The feeling is awesome.

Promoting mutual understanding across the walls of diverse groups for the sake of facilitating love is an honorable objective, not for the welling up of good feelings, but because doing so is morally right, and avoiding doing so is morally wrong.

As a deaf or hearing person, your life was changed on July 26, 1990. The United States Congress and President George Herbert Walker Bush saw to that when jointly they passed into law, and subsequently enacted, Public Law 101-336, the Americans with Disabilities Act. How drastically your life was changed depends, I guess, on how recognizable your disability is to the three branches of our federal government.

5

The parade of people with *acknowledged* disabilities seems to be led by those in wheelchairs, while the trailing unit of the cortege is comprised of the ranks of the deaf. While I do not in any way intend to rain on this parade, I will share with you my observation that most of the acknowledging of who is disabled, and who isn't, is done by people who are clueless about living with any of the acknowledged differences. And besides, I have never met anyone without some sort of challenge in life, some deficiency somewhere, some baggage hauled in from the family of origin that could have made life less cumbersome if said baggage had been checked through to the final destination.

We are all somewhat restricted, disabled, codependent, deprived, depraved, challenged. (*This promenade of currently fashionable adjectives is longer than the procession of people they describe.*) So the Americans with Disabilities Act is an early attempt to legislate sensitivity with response into the populace *en masse*. Most of the people I know refer to the Americans with Disabilities Act as the ADA, so, in this writing, I will use either term.

The ADA has affected your life and mine radically, moderately, subtly, or subliminally. We have ramps everywhere: on our street corners, campuses, building entrances. The bumps of Braille are on restroom doors, in elevators, and at the gym on the flat electronic keyboard that tells my workout machine how much to resist me.

Hotel rooms have methods for the hearing impaired to order room service, receive telephone calls and messages, and be awakened at a desired time.

Televisions have devices to display captioned dialog—and other sounds. (*How does anyone effectively caption a sound for a person who has never heard a sound?*)

Deaf people are now granted "access" to conversation and communication with hearing people in hospitals, doctors' offices and other medical places, in courts and government offices, and in schools, colleges, and universities. Sign language and sign language interpreters seem to be the all the rage these days. Signing pops up everywhere.

As Americans, or otherwise, living in the United States, we probably are more aware of people's special needs now than before ADA came to life. I applaud the legislation that created ADA; however, I am more impressed by the person whose mind, having become aware of the needs of others, responds to those needs with a sensitive heart instead of a legal shove.

Some Things I've Learned About Interpreting

As a way to get our feet wet regarding our topic, here is a list of some things I've learned about interpreting. I've become aware of this information from different places. Some things I've learned from observation, others from the gracious teachings of deaf people, a few from books and courses, and some from other interpreters. Please keep in mind these conclusions are mine only. I'm not asking that you draw the same conclusions. Use these concise, clipped considerations not as remarks of declared fact, but rather as springboards for thought and as springboards for the following chapters in this book. (*For a broad-ranged overview of deafness and deaf culture, I recommend a book by Matthew S. Moore and Linda Levitan,* For Hearing People ONLY, *published by Deaf Life Press, Rochester, New York.*)

(1) The greatest single impediment that results from not being able to hear is the barrier to language learning which, in turn, is the main reason for educational blockage. When hearing children enter school at five or six years of age, they have already acquired a rich background of heard language absorbed gradually from the day of birth. The language they have learned is the same language the teachers will use at school. The congenitally deaf child is denied this experience. Enter: the interpreter — but not to save the day — or the deaf. Rather we're there to facilitate communication as much as we can.

(2) In college classrooms (*except at Gallaudet University in Washington, D.C., a university for the deaf*) most deaf students will use an interpreter. The presence of an interpreter enables the deaf student to understand what is being said (*most of the time!*). "Oral" interpreters mouth what is being said. "Manual" interpreters use sign language. The two methods are often used in combination. A lag time exists between the spoken word and the expression of the interpretation. The length of the lag time varies depending on the situation. Thus, a deaf or hard of hearing student's contribution to the lecture or discussion will be slightly delayed.

(3) Many of us interpreters have been taught that we should be fluent, flawless signing machines devoid of opinions, feelings, or desires for relationships. We

are, of course, human. For many of us, ASL is not our native language. Deaf people can fly by most of us with their fluency of ASL leaving us in their dust any time they want. No matter how advanced our skill level, we sometimes make mistakes, forget signs, botch our fingerspelling, and become confused in our lag time. We occasionally have strong opinions about the topics or statements we're interpreting. We are emotional creatures. I have personally ridden the range of feelings while interpreting. My eyes have moistened with sympathy during sensitive moments. I have laughed and have felt frustration and anger. And we inevitably develop some kind of connection with the people who use our services. Interpreters should strive to express accurately the content and tone of the message we're interpreting and behave appropriately to the moment. At the same time your acknowledging that we are present—in our humanness—provides comfort and relieves stress to all involved. Communication clarity is thereby enhanced.

(4) Can your eyes focus on two different objects at once? How well can you drink in two fields of view simultaneously? A hearing student can study a diagram, an art project, a board of algebra equations, a beaker of reacting chemicals, a blueprint, or a graded test paper *and* listen to the teacher's comments at the same time. A deaf student has great difficulty doing this. Because the deaf student "listens" by watching the interpreter, "listening" and looking requires his being in two visual places concurrently. Solving this dilemma is a matter of remembering a couple of considerations presented in Chapter 5. Notably the use of these simple techniques benefits the hearing students too!

(5) Some deaf students are culturally separated or isolated to various degrees. Deaf culture is a separate subculture within our society with its own language, traditions, attitudes, values, jokes, and view of life. Not all deaf people choose to associate closely with this culture, but many do. If an individual has associated almost exclusively with the deaf community and has not related much with the hearing community, culturally-based misunderstandings can occur within the college environment just as they might with a new immigrant from another country. Interpreters attempt to bridge this cultural gap by using a method of interpreting called bilingual-bicultural (*BiBi*).

(6) My interpreting professors taught me that some things can't be interpreted from English to ASL or from ASL to English. They were right. (*Chapter 3 deals with many of these gnarly things.*) I believe that most deaf people understand this concept well. I think that most hearing people, especially the monolingual ones, are unaware that interpreters can't interpret some things. If the deaf and the hearing were sensitive to the interpreter's predicament at such moments, everybody would understand why everybody doesn't understand everything.

(7) American Sign Language (*ASL*) is, indeed, a language. Linguists have analyzed it and declared it so. We who use it are aware it is a language in its own right. ASL has its own alphabet, vocabulary, syntax, grammar, "word" order, idioms, registers, slang, and regional variations with local characteristics. Like any other language, ASL is in a constant state of change. It adopts new signs as others become archaic and fade from usage. It embraces all fields of technology, e.g.,

medicine, computer science, religion, mathematics —
you name it. ASL can be used for stories, poetry,
songs, casual conversation, religious liturgies, technical
lectures — for anything languages can express. ASL has
its own puns, nuances, amphiboly and wordplay
(*ah...signplay*). It can be used to swear at people with
vulgarities, to taunt, to hurt, to injure, or it can be used
to express love and friendship, to build up and encourage, to comfort, or to exalt. ASL can be mumbled,
droned, stammered, and butchered or expressed with
marvelous fluidity and articulation. ASL is employable
in any sort of situation or circumstance — a functional,
valuable, and truly beautiful treasure.

Who owns this valuable treasure? I have read, and
my deaf friends have let me know, that ASL belongs to
the deaf. It is the language of the deaf, for the deaf.
Furthermore, the deaf have implied exclusive rights to
preserve it and protect it from corruption, to teach it,
and define how it is correctly used. They claim their
language is the basis of the deaf culture and a source of
pride for the deaf community.

Please allow me to present an addition to these
thoughts in an attempt to break down some walls.
Surely, ASL is at least one basis for the deaf culture. To
my knowledge, no culture or subculture springs or
oozes into existence or survives without a common
language or a specialized edition of a common language. (*Look to American teenagers, their subculture
and their specialization of American English.*) For the
deaf in America, ASL is that common language. Therefore the deaf have the strongest motivation to guard
ASL from corruption and influences that would de-

11

mean it. I believe the job is theirs and rightfully should be.

But wait a minute. Be careful here. Before any of us conclude forever that ASL belongs to the deaf and that the deaf are the sole legal guardians of ASL, please ponder the following observations and opinions:

(1) Not all hearing Americans speak American English well. Some wallow daily in the muck of lousy grammar and vulgarities without knowing better. Yet, I suppose, they consider themselves fluent in their native language. Colorful, perhaps; fluent, by no means. I certainly do not want these linguistic butchers to serve as the "Grammar Answer Authorities" for American English.

Conversely, I have seen some—more than a few— deaf-from-birth people sign ASL atrociously. Should they be the torchbearers for correct ASL usage just because they are deaf? If not they, then who should carry the ASL language torch from dark spot to dark spot?

Just as some deaf people voice and write English more correctly than some monolingual English users, so do some hearing people sign ASL more correctly and expressively than do some deaf people. Perhaps then, the correctness of ASL expression should be determined by grammatical and syntactical standards and by global usage, but not by any one group's usage. ASL is best standardized, guarded, and taught by those who respect it, cherish its history and tradition, study and marvel at its varied beauty, and sign it with all of the delicate articulation of its expressive power. *These* people should influence ASL whether they be hearing or deaf.

12

(2) Many deaf people have told me that ASL is the language of the deaf, and it belongs to the deaf. Perhaps this is the prevailing concept in the deaf community. Yes, the deaf in America use ASL, but so do hearing people. I have had eleventeen zillion ASL conversations with other hearing people, and I continue to use ASL regularly for various desirable and useful reasons. *(I was recently in an airport coffee shop in Seattle with another interpreter. As we talked in English over breakfast we noticed that customers at nearby tables were being approached by a hearing person with survey sheets and a handful of golf pencils. We switched languages from English to ASL, and the solicitor passed us by. Another hearing man we didn't know, who was sitting alone, was approached instead. After listening to the spiel from the lady with the pencils, he took the survey, then signed to us in fluent ASL that he thought our language switch was clever. He wished we had included him! On another occasion, I was with a fellow interpreter in a restaurant booth. We were conversing in English when a lady in the adjoining booth turned around and told us she felt compelled to comment on our conversation. We listened politely, then immediately switched languages to ASL. For the next 45 minutes, she never heard another word from us!)* Hearing people are certainly allowed to use ASL. Languages do not belong to any group of people. No one owns a language. Languages, including ASL, are a part of the public domain. Anyone who wants to use a language and knows how may do so. Attaining a specified skill level is not required. One doesn't need to obtain a license or certificate. One simply uses a language as best he can. For anyone who believes the deaf have exclusive rights to ASL, to use it, to standardize it, to teach it, I recommend you regard

ASL as a magnificent gift for all willing to learn to use it. Such regard would crack one more barrier wall between the hearing and the deaf.

(3) "ASL is a source of pride to the deaf community," say many deaf people. If pride means unashamed pleasure in using ASL anywhere and in front of anyone, that is a thing to be desired. But for some, pride in ASL seems to be a covetous clinging to the language, a Mine!-Mine!- Mine! attitude. Perhaps this posture, this disposition is a compensation for an era recently past when ASL was rarely used by the deaf in public. ASL's public use was somehow considered a stigma, something that drew unwanted attention. The oral schools reinforced the notion. If the pride and the display of ASL is a means of swaggering revenge and parading the thrill of victory over those bygone days, I pray we allow those feelings to melt away. Some people believe pride is a positive possession. I believe the opposite. Pride has little use except to show up shortly before destruction. Pride is the buttress that keeps the wall between us in place. Pride is an abomination to a loving, understanding relationship. In pride's absence, we can have interactive relationships with mutual respect, understanding, sharing, and love. Pride in a school, or a baseball team, or a language is a concept far inferior to the unity we so desperately need. Oh that we could share in each other's lives instead of boasting with the pride of our own. Puffed-up strutting behind a wall of separation is as self-deceiving as it is ludicrous. Could we please consider that ASL is a blessing or a treasure or a gem or a source of joy to the deaf community instead of a source of pride? The reconsidering of the pride concept and the subsequent changing of our words and signs may seem a small

14

point. The smallest amount of light drives back the greatest amount of darkness.

"The best way to see divine light is to put out thy own candle."

—Thomas Fuller, M.D

"Imparting knowledge is only lighting another man's candle at our lamp, without depriving ourselves of any flame."

—Jane Porter

CHAPTER 2

No, Sign Language is Not Universal

(The Nature of Signed Communication)

The purpose of this chapter is to give people who are unfamiliar with manual-visual communication (*sign language*) an overview, a synopsis of what is really going on when people are signing to each other. A thumbnail glimpse of sign language is enchanting; an in-depth study is enthralling. *(I encourage a more penetrating study of ASL if you have even a small impulse to probe deeper.)* Here are nine questions and answers about sign language placed here to give you a basic, general understanding of signed communication. Knowing this information will help you communicate through an interpreter.

Is sign language universal?

No, sign language is not universal. American Sign Language has its own alphabet, although the ASL alphabet is used in the sign languages of some other countries. (*When I visited the Uganda School for the Deaf in Entebbe, I learned they use Ugandan Sign Language signs, but they fingerspell with the ASL alphabet.*) ASL has its own grammar and syntax, idioms, slang, and other components. American Sign Language is very different from and independent of American English. For example, ASL has no form of the verb *to be*, has no definite or indefinite articles (*a, an, the*) and no verb tenses. Of course, ASL has all of the syntactical tools necessary to express fully any meanings, concepts, or nuances available to English users. Various countries all over the world have their own sign languages. ASL varies in usage, vocabulary, and expression from region to region in the United States. Dialects and accents vary even from Southern California to Northern California. (*I live and work in California. I once interpreted for a deaf student from New York. Because of his accent, I labored and sometimes struggled to understand his ASL.*)

Let me take a pause from our overview of ASL to answer the second most frequently asked question I hear about sign language: Well, if sign language isn't universal, why not? Why doesn't someone just come up with a generic, worldwide version? Wouldn't that make sense, make things a lot easier? Actually that's been tried. An artificial international sign language called Gestuno was created and has been used at some international deaf conferences (*or so I've been told*). An artificial international spoken (*oral-aural*) language called Esperanto was invented by L.L. Zamenhof. I've never met anyone who uses either one of these languages. I think they will never catch on. Languages are alive. They are constantly changing and developing. The meaning of words and signs change over the years. New words and signs are perpetually being added. Technical words and signs, slang, jargon, and argot are forever entering and leaving a language. Consequently, one doesn't "just come up with" a language, sign or otherwise. Besides, how would you respond if someone suggested to you to give up your native language—the one you've used all your life—and switch to a new global language just because it makes sense? Enough said.

Is ASL really a language?

Yes, ASL is a living and fully-developed language and has been so declared by linguists. Linguists hesitated to give ASL the status of "language" for some time because ASL had no written form. ASL does now have a written form albeit contrived. (*I've never seen anyone curl up in front of a cozy fire with a novel written in ASL. I think that will never happen.*) ASL is a deeply-rich, fully-developed, beautifully-expressive language independent of any written form.

Giving hearing instructors and hearing students some insight into the nature of ASL and ASL's relationship to American English should provide more girders to help bridge the communication gap between the hearing and the deaf.

Is ASL just visual English?

No, ASL is technically (*linguistically*) independent of American English, but the two languages do have a relationship. American English has a definite influence on ASL. (*French Sign Language, from which American Sign Language was birthed, and the French language have had significant linguistic influences on ASL.*)

Each of the 26 English letters of the alphabet is represented by a different hand shape in ASL. (*Actually the I and the J are the same hand shape, but the movement is different. The G and Q, the H and U, and the K and P as pairs share the same shape, but their positions are different.*) The ASL alphabet is used by signers to fingerspell proper nouns and other specific English words. (*Fingerspelling is technically known as* **dactology** *or sometimes* **dactylology,** *although I've never actually heard anyone use those words in a conversation or lecture.*) In a classroom setting if a specific English word is important for the student to know, I will fingerspell the word. If the word is spoken repeatedly the deaf student and I will agree on a sign for that word. (*In that case the sign will represent the English* word **and** *its concept, not just the concept itself.*)

Is there an ASL sign for every English word?

No, ASL signs express concepts. They do not represent English words. For example, the ASL sign used to express the color of the sky, does not represent the English word *blue*. The sign expresses the universal concept of blueness. Because an interpreter would almost always voice the word *blue* when interpreting that sign, *blue* is known as the gloss word for that sign. The sign with the gloss word *hello* could be interpreted *howdy* because the interpreter expresses the concept with the English word most appropriate for the context. Therefore English and ASL do not lend themselves to translation of each other (*gloss-for-gloss*) but rather to interpretation (*concept-for-concept*). Knowing this would help one understand why a deaf student's receiving a lecture in ASL and then being tested on the information in written English may generate some difficulties.

Do ASL signs look like the concepts they represent?

Yes, sometimes they do, and no, quite often they do not. Signs that look like the concepts they represent are called iconic signs. Many of the signs for specific animal species, the shapes of items, and the physical descriptions of people are iconic. Other signs have known etymologies but are not iconic at all.

What are initialized signs?

ASL signs have three (*and very often four*) components: shape, location, movement (*and facial expression*). Altering any of the components will almost always alter the meaning. The hand shape of some ASL signs is the ASL letter of the alphabet that corresponds to the English letter that begins that sign's gloss word. For example, the sign for "emergency" is formed with the "e" hand shape. Such signs are called initialized signs.

Why do interpreters and other ASL users seem to exaggerate their facial expressions?

Facial expressions are a required component and an integral part of ASL. Facial expressions are to ASL

21

what voice intonation is to English. If an English speaker says, "I'm depressed," with a cheerful voice, a mixed message is sent. If an ASL user signs, "I'm sad," with a giddy facial expression, not only is the message confused but the ASL grammar is incorrect. Because facial expressions are crucial to ASL, they often are given emphasis to ensure the meaning is clear. Non-ASL users sometimes think interpreters' facial expressions are exaggerated because facial emphasis is unusual in the hearing world. Watch two hearing people in conversation and you will probably see two deadpan faces gazing at each other with only lips moving.

In ASL, facial expressions required to express meaning are referred to as facial grammar. For example, when asking a question that can be answered yes or no, the signer's eyebrows are to be raised. When asking a question that cannot be answered yes or no — e.g.: "What is your name?" — the signer is to lower the eyebrows below their relaxed position. Sometimes the facial expression or head movement can change the meaning of things drastically. A head movement can change a statement from a positive sense to a negative one or change the meaning of the sign for "anyway" to "never mind." Instructors: don't be alarmed that the interpreter's facial and sometimes body expressions are vivid. It's all part of the language.

Is there more than one American sign language?

No, linguistically there is only one American sign *language* with its regional and individual variations. There are, however, several manual communication systems that have been contrived by various people.

The signs of these systems are designed to represent English words and grammar exactly as it is spoken. Signs are available for English suffixes and prefixes. In these systems many signs are initialized. Some systems pay little attention to joining a sign with a concept, but link the sign instead to phonetics. For example, the sign for the word *sink* would be the same if the concept is "the kitchen sink" or "the boat will sink." These sign systems were designed, ostensibly, to help deaf children learn English in the early grades. The success of the systems is debated. The use of the systems is a source of much consternation in the deaf community. Three of the systems are: (1) SEE I—Seeing Essential English, David Anthony's visual English system that requires English words that are pronounced the same to have one common sign; (2) SEE II—Signing Exact English, a manual code for English originated by Gustason, Pfetzing, and Sawalkow that tries to achieve a one-to-one correspondence between English words or syllables and a single sign for each word or syllable; and (3) L.O.V.E.—Linguistics of Visual English developed by Wampler in 1972. These systems, and others like them, are collectively referred to as Manually Coded English (*MCE*).

So, what do interpreters do? Do they know ASL and all of the systems, or do they specialize, or what?

The answer to this question is not simple. ASL and MCE can be placed on opposite ends on a manual communication continuum.

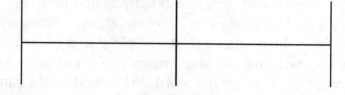

ASL   CASE   MCE

The sign language interpreting program that certified me required 32 units of classes in which I was taught American Sign Language, its vocabulary, grammar, syntax, number systems (*There are 14!*), and styles. I had to pass countless exams interpreting English to ASL and ASL to English. In two class meetings of one advanced interpreting class I was taught a Manually Coded English system. I was required to pass one exam interpreting English to SEE II.

Not surprisingly, I tend to interpret on the ASL end of the continuum. Interpreters who work in the lower grades tend to work (*and in many classrooms are required to work*) on the MCE end of the continuum. I consider myself an ASL interpreter although I may occasionally use some MCE signs.

The interpreters I know who work at the college level hover around the middle of the continuum and use Conceptually Accurate Signed English or CASE. (*CASE is sometimes called PIDGIN sign language, a term I disdain and don't use.*) CASE is the use of ASL signs in English word order. The use of CASE allows the interpreter to mouth the English gloss words or alternate English words and sign at the same time. This practice is an advantage to most deaf students.

If an interpreter is competent and versatile, that interpreter can set up his home base at any point on the continuum. Oftentimes the deaf client has a preference for ASL, CASE, or MCE. If both the deaf student and the interpreter can glide smoothly along the continuum, communication is enhanced.

One more concept needs to be presented here that should serve to bring a conclusion to our considerations. That concept is one that has come to be known as Total Communication. Total Communication is an eclectic method of communicating with the hearing impaired that employs the use of all other communication methods available including signing, speech reading, fingerspelling, residual aural capabilities, gesturing, and even writing. The Total Communication method essentially means the interpreter can do whatever is efficient to make the communication happen. Just how Total Communication is used depends on the preferences and needs of the deaf student and the skills of the interpreter.

Instructors for whom I interpret: please know that while I work most of the time between ASL and CASE on the continuum, I am an advocate of Total Communication. I will do whatever I have to do to make the spoken (*or sometimes written*) communication clear to the deaf student. I have done such things as sit or stand alongside the deaf student to point to places on a test or paper being discussed. I have summarized points in lectures spoken forth too fast to be understood word-for- word. I have been known to stop signing the lecture to help a student step-by-step through an algebra problem as the instructor guides. I have asked note takers, during lectures, if they jotted down the terms the instructor just mentioned. Total Communication is a ray of light, an approval for interpreters to do whatever is necessary to get the job done. Instructors should have no concern if I or my fellow interpreters depart from conventional interpreting procedure to interact with the deaf student in an unconventional way.

What is really going on when people communicate face-to-face without voices? When the thought of one mind arrives intact in another's mind having traveled from the muscles of arms and hands and face through two eyes, a complex and beautiful transaction has occurred. American Sign Language is a living treasure to be respected and protected, and to be used with dignity and enjoyment.

"*I hold myself indebted to anyone from whose enlightened understanding another ray of knowledge communicates to mind. Really to inform the mind is to correct and enlarge the heart.*"

—Julius

"The light shines in the darkness, but the darkness has not understood it."

—The Bible, John 1:17

CHAPTER 3

Say What?

(Linguistic Interpreting Difficulties)

Some vocal stuff is really tough to sign especially if the speaker is expounding at a breakneck pace.

"The Rotogravure printing press was able to display beautifully the trumpeting African elephant wrestling with the giraffe on the swampy rain forest floor."

"Okay now what I'm gonna do is, I'm gonna go ahead and, I think I'm gonna proceed now with taking another look at, uh, er, review last week's lesson."

"Y = 1/X has an asymptote when X = 0. This means the graph kisses the asymptote." **(By the time I finished explaining to the deaf student what was funny, why this gem caused so much laughter in the classroom, I was hopelessly behind.)**

This chapter is about formulations people speak that interpreters must sign, things teachers and students come out with that have put some grey hair on this interpreter's head. From the onset, let me state that never for one short moment would I ever suggest that a hearing speaker or a deaf signer should alter his method of expression. *(When you read on you will discover a couple of exceptions.)* Bringing precise understanding from one language and culture to another is the interpreter's responsibility. Meeting these linguistic challenges is *my* responsibility — and onus. My goal in this chapter is to present some of the perplexities of interpreting English to ASL. Then you may understand why sometimes your interpreter's hands are clenched and frozen. It's because my brain is scanning itself for a way to express what I think I perceive. These speakers' foibles insert speed bumps on the path to smooth and comfortable understanding. These undesirable speaker patterns are sometimes called "speaker miscues." Such speaker behaviors might include false starts, mispronunciations, inappropriate intonation patterns, errors in lexical selection, ungrammatical sentence structures, ambiguous referencing, and other misconstructions such as spoonerisms.

I have categorized these bothersome linguistic quandaries into three groups: (1) sound and word-choice difficulties, (2) reference difficulties, and (3) culture difficulties.

Sound and Word-Choice Difficulties

Some spoken concepts are troublesome to interpret into ASL because their meaning is dependent on the way the English sounds as it is uttered. A pun is an example. The meaning of another kind of spoken expression in this category requires the listener to know the difference between the proper use of English and its improper use. The improper use may be intended or unintended by the speaker. A malapropism is an example.

Here are a few sound and word-choice difficulties and some comments:

PUNS
(*Paronomasia*)

A pun is the use of a word or phrase to emphasize its different meanings or uses *or* the use of words that are alike in sound but different in meaning. I once had to interpret, "When Johnny Appleseed fed the animals he was getting to the core of his interest." Another example is "That jobless man makes no sense (*cents*)." Because the double or multiple meanings exist in English only and not in ASL, the interpreter is forced to express one of the concepts in sign, then express the other(s), and then explain the pun. (*All this, of course, assumes (1) that the interpreter understands all of the meanings and (2) that there is enough time to sign everything.*) Sometimes the deaf person will be "English" enough to understand the pun without an explanation, but oftentimes that isn't the case.

MUMBLE

Some hearing English speakers don't articulate or enunciate well. Both of our grown sons, Brent and Chad, can speak fluent mumble at will, and they can understand, so it seems, any speech utterance: deaf speech, teenage talk, rap and any other musical lyrics, drunk babble, and indistinct splutter. Brent can even understand the speech-and-static noise that explodes forth from fast-food, drive-through speakers! I'm not so gifted. In an interpreting situation, when I don't understand the speaker, I will sign that I cannot understand the speech or I will interrupt the speaker and ask him to repeat himself. Which of the two I choose to do depends on etiquette, protocol, prudence, and other good-sense assessments of the circumstance.

MALAPROPISM

A malapropism is a misapplication of a word, specifically the use of a word sounding somewhat like the one intended but ludicrously wrong or slightly wrong in the context. Mrs. Malaprop was a character noted for her misuse of words in R.B. Sheridan's 1775 comedy play, *The Rival*. I heard Dr. Bob Ferguson, a psychology professor at Saddleback College, quoting a person with histrionic personality disorder, say, "I'm a veterinarian. I don't eat meat." Another classic example of a malapropism is "Lead the way and we'll precede." Malapropisms are tricky to interpret. I almost always provide an exclamation in ASL. (*Sorry*)

METONYMY

Metonymy is a figure of speech in which one word or phrase is used for another with which it is closely associated. For example, instead of saying, "The President in Washington expressed anger at the government in Russia," one might say, "The White House rattled its saber at the Kremlin." The language is colorful, but the meaning for some people is sometimes gray. Many metonymies in one setting will fatigue an interpreter who must hack through a jungle of flowery vines.

ANADIPLOSIS

An anadiplosis is a rhetorical repetition at the beginning of a phrase, a repetition of the word or words with which the previous phrase ended. A couple of examples are (1) "Rely on his honor—honor such as his?" and (2) "Soon I'm going to test your skills, your skills I say, in due time." Interpretation here doesn't involve double meanings, but keep in mind that in an anadiplosis the word repeated is pronounced the second time louder and stronger that the first. Interpreters should express the emphasis.

SPOONERISMS

Spoonerisms are a kick. They are the transposition of the initial sounds of words, usually by accident. Some linguists refer to spoonerisms as reversal errors. An example is "the queer old dean" when what is meant is "the dear old queen." Once, while teaching *Exodus*, I said, "pent teg" but I meant "tent peg."

There once lived an English clergyman named W.A. Spooner (*1844-1930*) who was known for such slips. The mistakes are named for him. (*What a distinction!*) His interpreter should be canonized having had to deal with "tons of soil" for "sons of toil" and the like. I once heard someone say, "Little Hood Riding Red went to her mangruther with a gasket of boodies." !!

Interpreting spoonerisms is impossible. I just fingerspell the mistakes and explain to the deaf person what happened—if time permits. The nonvocal deaf people I know don't understand spoonerisms at all, why and how they happen or why they're funny. I don't understand why and how they happen either. I do know that mine are embarrassing and everyone else's are funny.

POEMS

Poems, especially verse that depends on rhyme or the sounds of English words for meaning, can be practically impossible to interpret without explanation to the deaf student. (*The explanation, of course, ruins the fluidity or rhythmic beauty of the poem.*) Limericks are good examples.

There once was a lady from Hyde,

Who ate a green apple and died.

While her lover lamented,

The apple fermented,

and made cider inside her inside.

(I can't give credit to the author by name; I have no idea who wrote it.)

KNOCK-KNOCK JOKES

The technical linguistic rhetorical label escapes me. The knock-knock joke, a questionably amusing phenomenon exclusive to hearing people, is another tough job for the interpreter.

> Knock knock.
>
> Who's there?
>
> Ether.
>
> Ether who?
>
> Ether bunny's on his way.
>
> Knock knock.
>
> Who's there?
>
> Orange.
>
> Orange who?
>
> Orange you glad I'm not the ether bunny?

> Knock knock
>
> Who's there?
>
> Cantaloupe.
>
> Cantaloupe who?
>
> Cantaloupe without a significant other.

Three or four of these in rapid sequence is enough to make an interpreter a little squirrelly.

ONOMATOPOEIA

Onomatopoeia is the formation of a word by initiations of a sound made by or associated with its referent. Roughly then, these are words that sound like what they mean. Examples are *buzz, murmur, swish, boom,* and *cuckoo.* They are very tough to interpret if the speaker uses the words to denote their referent concepts. If, however, the speaker pronounces them as a sound effect, I explain that to the deaf student as best I can.

SHAKESPEARE

Shakespeare's works, read or performed, present huge difficulties for an interpreter — at least for me. I'm no expert here (*maybe that's part of the problem*) but it seems the character and much of the appeal of Shakespeare's plays is found in the sounds of the Elizabethan English as they roll from the tongues and lips of the actors. If I can understand the meaning of William Shakespeare's words, metaphors, similes, idioms, and other tools of expression, I can usually interpret the wisdom, drama, and wit of his plays. I am still at a loss to convey the flavor of his language in ASL. *What manner or make of men are these who wear their balls in parenthesis?* definitely loses something, in addition to the rhyme, in translation. *What kind of men are bowlegged?* doesn't quite get the job done. (*I think that first line above is not really Shakespeare, but I DID have to interpret it once.*)

I'll cap my point here with this exercise for my fellow interpreters. Ask someone to read, at a normal

speaking pace, Brabantio's lines from OTHELLO: 1:2
and you interpret what you hear.

O thou foul thief, where hast thou stowed my
daughter?

Damned as thou art, thou hast enchanted her!

For I'll refer me to all things of sense,

If she in chains of magic were not bound

Whether a maid so tender, fair, and happy,

So opposite to marriage that she shunned

The wealthy curlèd darlings of our nation,

Would ever have, t' incur a general mock,

Run from her guardage to the sooty bosom

Of such a thing as thou—to fear, not to delight.

Judge me the world if 'tis not gross in sense

That thou hast practiced on her with foul
charms,

Abused her delicate youth with drugs or miner-
als

That weakens motion. I'll have 't disputed on;

'Tis probable, and palpable to thinking.

I therefore apprehend and do attach thee

For an abuser of the world, a practicer

Of arts inhibited and out of warrant.

Lay hold upon him! If he do resist,

Subdue him at his peril.

How did you do? Don't despair if you struggled. I believe we all do.

My method for dealing with Shakespeare in a classroom includes:

(1) discussing the interpreting problems with the student and the instructor beforehand

(2) helping the deaf student follow classroom readings by pointing in his text to the lines being read

(3) encouraging the student to read and become very familiar with a play before the video is shown in class

(4) interpreting the video showings using ASL signs, concepts, and mood disregarding only Elizabethan English considerations.

Of course the video showings have their own inherent problem: the deaf student attempts to watch the video and the interpreter at the same time.

BEST WISHES, EVERYONE!

SOUND CONCEPTS

Sometimes lecturers present topics the understanding of which requires a group of sound-related concepts. Many deaf people have no experiential familiarity with such notions. Musical terms, for example, represent only abstractions to most of my deaf clients. How meaningful to a person who has never heard music would these terms be: *melody, harmony, treble, bass, dissonance, diminished seventh, resolving triad,* or *minor key?* ASL signs that portray characteristics of sounds are understandably few and far between and seldom seen. Teachers should remember that using metaphors, similes, or other illustrations containing sound concepts is probably not the clearest way to make a point with a deaf person.

ANTICIPATION ERROR

Anticipation error happens when a sound or word is brought forward in a sentence and used before it is needed. An example is *I'll put your c̲at in the c̲loset* instead of *I'll put your hat in the closet.*

PERSEVERATION ERROR

Perseveration error occurs when a sound or word that has already been spoken is repeated. An example is *the p̲resident of P̲rance* instead of *the president of France.* Anticipation and perseveration mistakes are somewhat common but are not serious for an interpreter. They will probably cause a momentary stumble and will be corrected if the speaker makes the correction. If the speaker doesn't correct himself, I probably won't make the correction either unless the deaf student expresses confusion. Then, if time permits, I will explain what I believed happened.

SPEECH RATE

A speaker can possibly utter so many words per minute that an interpreter can't keep up, especially if the speed rate is overaggressive for a sustained period. A skilled interpreter should be able to keep up at a fairly brisk clip, but everyone has a max speed. A speaker's rate will usually increase dramatically when reading aloud. Students who read reports to the class have the swiftest, most accelerated speech because of nervousness and because no creative linguistic mental processes are required when reading. When interpreting for these speedsters, I simply interrupt them and ask them to slow down. The speakers have always acknowledged my request, but not all comply. By the way, I don't hesitate to ask for a slower rate in a classroom. I would *never* make such an appeal on a stage with an audience present, during a church service, in a court room, or the like. Prudence reigns.

ACCENTS AND DIALECTS

I report accents and dialects — as I perceive them — to the deaf student. For example I may sign *French accent* or *heavy Spanish accent* or *seems like a Boston dialect* or *very high-pitched voice*, or *he is stuttering (or some other speech impediment)*. I do this because the dialect or accent the speaker expresses is linguistic information available to the hearing listener. If the deaf person is aware of an accent, especially a thick one, he will then understand the reason I may not catch all of what is being said. Whatever else he does with his awareness of an accent or dialect or an unusual vocal characteristic is up to him.

One danger here is that the interpreter's report to the deaf client is highly subjective, therefore I try to be careful with my phrasing. I would likely say, for instance, "His accent seems like Minnesota." (*ASL wording*) I would not say, "I think he's from Minnesota." The practice of mentioning distinctive speech qualities deviates from my formal interpreter training, but I believe doing so can sometimes be beneficial to the deaf.

The above list of fifteen sound and word-choice difficulties I encounter while interpreting is probably not exhaustive, but it should give hearing speakers and deaf listeners some insight into the occasional quizzical looks on my face.

Reference Difficulties

This category of reference difficulties involves confusions of concepts instead of confusions linked with sounds. Let me give you nine classifications in this category with examples of each.

GOLDWYNISMS

Named for Samuel Goldwyn (*whose original name was Goldfish*), a goldwynism is a phrase or expression involving a grotesque use of a word, e.g.: *include me out*. Here is another example I believe would qualify: *The pigeon owner flew the coop on TWA.*

ANTHONYISMS

Ralph T. Anthony and I were in the U.S. navy at the same time. We encountered each other at Great Lakes Naval Training Center. He said so many strange and confusing things—that, for a split second, seemed to make sense—I called them anthonyisms. Some linguists refer to this kind of remark as Irish Bull. These statements are an apparently congruous but actually incongruous expression like *It was hereditary in his family to have no children.* I once heard myself say, "Work hard at getting a good rest." During one chatty afternoon with Ralph T. Anthony I asked, "Anthony, what does the *T* stand for?" "Why Jim, that's my middle initial." Another time talking about a group of officers who were always late, Anthony told me, "Sometimes when they get here they don't even show up."

YOGIES

Named for Lawrence Peter "Yogi" Berra, famous New York Yankee baseball player, these utterances have no technical definition of which I'm aware. All I can tell you is they sound weird, make sense if you think about them, cause an interpreter to do some quick mental tap dancing, and they don't come across from English into ASL very well at all. Below are 20 quotations attributed to Yogi Berra. (*I know 20 is overkill for purposes of illustration. I just like the quotes.*)

1. "It ain't over till it's over."

2. "This is like deja vu all over again."

3. Phil Rizzuto: "Hey Yogi, I think we're lost."

   Yogi Berra: "Ya, but we're making great time!"

4. "You better cut the pizza in four pieces because I'm not hungry enough to eat six."

5. "I couldn't tell if the streaker was a man or a woman because it had a bag on its head."

6. "You can observe a lot just by watchin'."

7. "In baseball, you don't know nothin'."

8. "How can you think and hit at the same time?"

9. Yogi Berra on seeing a Steve McQueen movie: "He must have made that before he died."

10. "If you can't imitate him, don't copy him."

11. "Baseball is 90% mental, the other half is physical."

12. Mrs. Lindsay: "You certainly look cool."

Yogi Berra: "Thanks, you don't look so hot yourself."

13. Nobody goes there anymore; it's too crowded."

14. I want to thank all those who made this night necessary."

15. I knew I was going to take the wrong train, so I left early."

16. Interviewer: "Why, you're a fatalist!"

Yogi Berra: "You mean I save postage stamps? Not me."

17. You got to be very careful if you don't know where you're going, because you might not get there."

18. "Slump?, I ain't in no slump. I just ain't hittin'."

19. "It's pretty far, but it doesn't seem like it."

20. "It was impossible to get a conversation going, everybody was talking too much."

While the original yogies are attributed to Yogi Berra, many other speakers have added creatively and unwittingly to this brand of strange sayings.

THIS AND THAT

"This and That" refers to the use of the expressions *this* and *that* and *over there* and *looks like these*, and the like used by instructors when they are lecturing and pointing to writing on the board. Math teachers are notorious for this practice. Pointing to something on the board and saying *this* and *that* requires the listener to look at the pointing in order to know the referent. A deaf student who is watching the interpreter (*who, of course, is lagging a few seconds behind the instructor*) must read the sign for *this* or *that* and quickly shift focus to the instructor. By the time that happens, the instructor is either finished pointing or is pointing to something else! A deaf student (*or any other student for that matter*) should not be expected to be visually in more than one place at the same time. I once interpreted for a math instructor who explained in this form: "If you divide this guy by that guy and raise him to the power of that guy over there, then your answer will be the square of this guy here." (*I pleaded with the teacher all semester to stop talking that way. "Oh pleeeeeeese don't do that," I begged. He never stopped, but he did later retire!*) This problem would end if the teachers used nouns instead of pronouns.

ANACOLUTHON

An anacoluthon is an abrupt change within a sentence to a second grammatical construction inconsistent with the first. Actually an anacoluthon is any grammatical construction involving a break in sequence or coherence like *It makes me so—I just get angry*. Another example is *He alerted her that if she*

44

turned left, what will happen to her? A type of ana-coluthon know as a false start is one I hear frequently from professors (!): *Okay, students, now today—what I want to do now is—I want you to get out a clean piece of paper to—you're going to have a quiz.* (**I interpret this with three signs: now, paper, quiz.**) Here is another representative illustration I've had to reckon with in classes I've worked. *Okay what I want you to do I we're not there's gonna be certain information . . . .*

WELLERISM

Wellerisms are named for Sam Weller or his father, a couple of celebrated characters in Dicken's "Pickwick Papers." Taking a familiar saying or proverb and applying it to an inappropriate situation, especially punningly or humorously, creates a wellerism. Here's one: *"Much noise and little wool,"* said the Devil when he sheared the pig. Many riddles are wellerisms. *What did one wall say to the other wall? "I'll meet you at the corner."*

CLOZE SKILLS (*Yep, with a z*)

Cloze skills require the listener to supply information not supplied by the speaker. An example: *If you do all of this, you will have finished the whole nine . . . .* That one is easy. The missing element is, of course, the word *yards.* If the speaker had said, "If you do all of this, you will have finished the whole . . . .", guessing the missing part is a harder puzzle. Should it be *the whole enchilada, the whole ball of wax, the whole thing,* or what? The more information the speaker omits, the more cognitive busywork is required of the listener and the sooner he will experience attention drift due to fatigue. Of more germane concern to interpreters is our role here. Should we take a stab at the absent phrase or should we too omit it? A purist would insist we sign only what has been spoken. If I believe I understand the concept the speaker intends to express, I will usually sign my interpretation to the deaf student letting him know that the speaker's expression was incomplete. I do this for two reasons: (1) unfinished spoken sentences tend to be esoteric to hearing American English users, thus hearing students and interpreters may be better equipped than the deaf student to surmise the fragment's meaning and (2) I am, after all, an interpreter, not a translator or transliterator, hence I interpret the meaning as I understand it.

ZEUGMAS

A zeugma is the use of one word in two constructions. Two examples are (1) a verb with two subjects or objects and (2) the use of an adjective with two nouns. A zeugma is created when a verb or preposition is applied to two other words in two different senses as in *she closed the door and her heart to her family.* Two of my favorite zeugmas are these: (1) "I just blew my nose, a fuse, and three circuit breakers" (Jim Henson), and (2) "Time flies like an arrow; fruit flies like a banana" (Groucho Marx). Some zeugmas are grammatically correct and others are grammatically wrong. All reduce syllables for the speaker and smooth flow for the interpreter. And that, my dear reader, was a zeugma.

AMBIGUOUS REFERENCING

Below is a sampling of Jabberwocky I've had to deal with in classes. Lumped here in an Ambiguous Referencing category, these utterances — shockingly from the mouths of professors — have all given me pause to ponder.

That's what Christianity is all about. (That's?)

Let's turn to—oh the class is running a little—that's okay...

... ya know you hear the original and maybe 20 seconds later you hear with your from your own voice.

... so that he could or she could know where he stood as in so far as language proficiency was concerned.

... because what is very easy at a given moment and have only three minutes of lengthy can become...

... and it had uh certain components into it...

...and the two things that we thought we could see in the performance was (sic) *the adaptability of the text and the other one being...*

Other types of reference difficulties are surely bouncing about unattached out there somewhere, but the above five classifications should give you an idea of what the brains of interpreters must process. I deal with reference problems in one of a couple ways. I can try to make sense of them, really sometimes just guessing (*interpret!*) what the speaker is trying to say and express my decision in ASL, or I can sign close to verbatim what the speaker said letting the deaf client try to make sense of it all.

God is quoted as saying (*The Bible, Genesis,* Chapter 11) regarding an idolatrous act of men, "'*If as one people speaking the same language they have begun to do this, then nothing they plan to do will be impossible for them. Come, let us go down and confuse their language so they will not understand each other.' That is why it* (**the tower they built and the place they built it**) *was called Babel—because there the Lord confused the language of the whole world.*" This so-called Curse of Babel has been tremendously successful!

Before we move on to cultural difficulties, I'd like to thank David Chapman, one of my fine, fine interpreting instructors, who said simply during one class, "Some things cannot be interpreted." What a load off my shoulders knowing that axiom the day I was interpreting in an English class at Saddleback College. The instructor read aloud a paragraph and exercise questions similar to the one below. I threw my hands in the air—ah, I mean put my hands in my lap—and surrendered. Interpreting this was beyond interpreting Shakespeare; it was an impossibility.

Reading Exercise

Instructions: Read the following paragraph and answer the questions with complete sentences.

The Pershor

The pershor was kining his trusp. Mebily a munz durpled some clan in his trusp. "Why did themp durp clav in my yulous trusp?" the pershor qurd the munz.

48

"A'nr linshily zergy," the munz xtrupped. "Gur beched themp pipeled clav in your trusp. Do themp kine your trusp yulous."

1. What was pershor kining?

2. What did the munz durp in the pershor's trusp?

3. What did the pershor qur the munz?

4. Was the munz zergy?

5. Who are the characters in the story?

All be aware: Some things cannot be interpreted.

Cultural Difficulties

Interpreting is obviously a bilingual activity. Interpreting back and forth between English and ASL is a bilingual *and* a bicultural undertaking. The deaf are the only group of people with a shared physical disability who have their own culture. (*See the Preface for some comments about the deaf culture and the use of the word* **disabled**.) I believe the deaf culture developed largely because of the deaf's use of American Sign Language. Secondarily, but significant, have been the contributions from deaf communities like Martha's Vineyard once was, from deaf schools such as Gallaudet University in Washington, D.C., and from clubs for the deaf all of which have provided venues for cultural development.

This section's purpose is not to describe the deaf culture per se but rather to inform that the deaf culture adds a dynamic to the communication interaction between the hearing and the deaf in general and to the interpreting process in particular. Knowing a little about this cultural dynamic should help us all understand why we don't always understand each other even with an interpreter.

The humor in the deaf culture, for example, is often based on visual concepts or on situations viewed from a uniquely deaf perspective. Sometimes deaf humor plays on ASL idioms or signs. All present difficulties for interpreters. Much of deaf humor doesn't transfer successfully to the hearing ear, and much hearing humor doesn't transfer successfully to the deaf.

One famous and very funny story told in ASL is that of a deaf King Kong climbing the outside of the Empire State Building looking for the beautiful woman he saw walking in through the front door. When King Kong discovers her through the window of an upper floor, he reaches in and pulls her to himself in the palm of his hand. Then, in ASL, he asks her to marry him. Of course, while asking this question, he crushes and kills her. The sign for *marry* involves thrusting both hands together, palm-to-palm, then both hands grasp each other. This story is hilarious in ASL, but nonsigning hearing people, even with voice interpretation, sit expressionless through the end of the joke.

Hearing people watch television, go to movies, and listen to the radio. Many deaf people watch television with captioning. A few go to movies, and none listen to the radio. Consequently the hearing become familiar with jingles, quips, catch phrases, characters, and so forth from the sound media. When hearing speakers make reference to such things, the deaf are generally left in the dark. If the deaf person asks the interpreter, "What does that mean? What's he talking about?" we have an interpreting problem. Bicultural interpreting requires that we interpreters bridge this cultural gap, so we give a brief explanation—as time allows—and keep on truckin'.

Instructors could help by selecting illustrations and references that are not esoteric to the hearing.

Many other characteristics peculiar to the deaf culture may cause interpreting difficulties. A study of the deaf culture is beyond our scope here. A hearing speaker's awareness of deaf culture's details and aspects is not expected by interpreters or deaf people. In summary, though, much would be gained in the college classroom if instructors would keep a couple of things in mind. When you are being interpreted you are, in essence, lecturing in two languages at the same time. Not every utterance is equally clear in both languages. If the English is sloppy and ambiguous, the ASL may be also. A skilled interpreter can make the ASL clearer than the English. Why, though, require an interpreter to clean up your linguistic, desultory mess? Clear, precise, well-structured English sentences are a blessing for the hearing and the deaf—and the interpreter!

"How far that little candle throws his beams!

So shines a good deed in a naughty world."

—William Shakespeare

> *"To be ignorant of one's igno-rance is the malady of the ignorant."*

—Amos Bronson Alcott

Chapter 4

Inquisition and Scrutiny

(Quizzes and Tests)

At the end of class the teacher, casual and de-tached, mentions, "Don't forget now, you're having a test on Monday." For the students, the weekend is wiped out, and the anxiety sets in. The amount of anxiety varies among the students. Some experience general uneasiness, worry, and feelings that shift be-tween urges to cram and tugging desires to give up. Others experience torrents of gushing adrenalin with undulating nausea, shooting chills, and disorienting dizziness. I'm sure some students, instead of taking a test, would prefer to make a speech on national televi-sion or flee from a snarling attacking pit bull.

In college, tests are inevitable, and the levels of fear and apprehension regarding them probably are too. The degree of test distress does vary from person to person. Assume for a moment that you are a student who learns quickly. For you, classroom material is easily assimilated. Math is fun, and you grasp that a hyperbola has two asymptotes passing through its center; and that an asymptote of a curve is a straight line with the property that the distance between it and the curve approaches zero as the curve recedes to infinity. A rectangular or equilateral hyperbola has asymptotes that are perpendicular to each other. You really do understand that! You can even solve this:

$$P(t) = \frac{L}{1 + ce^{-kt}}$$

The test wants you to use this formula to discover when the people of Rwanda will run out of food given a couple of furnished numbers, and you're not worried about how to calculate the answer. You catch and follow the concepts of history, psychology, and grammar. The electoral college, dissociative disorders, and the rule that possessive case always precedes gerunds are all constructs that instantly make perfect sense to you. You easily memorize word definitions. Of course, you're familiar with English, so you don't have much trouble discerning important distinctions of kindred terms. *(By the way, while we're on the subject of word distinctions, just to mention one of my own pet peeves, I've met at least seven psychology instructors, five with Ph.D.s in psychology, who don't distinguish the two terms* subconscious *and* unconscious. *They use them interchangeably. Freud himself went back and forth with these words! That creates an interpreting stumble. The two terms, it seems obvious to me, have different meanings, denotations, and connotations.* Subconscious *refers to activity in one's brain of which one is unaware, activity below the conscious level.*

Unconscious *would describe a person who is asleep, knocked out, under general anesthesia , and so on. Because the two words have distinctly different meanings, they are signed differently. I guess if the interpreter switches back and forth when the instructor does, it all evens out in the end. The deaf students are as confused as the hearing students!*) If you are a quick study and learning is easy, test taking is still probably a chore you'd just as soon skip.

Suppose, though, that learning isn't all that easy for you. Perhaps you've never correctly calculated how fast Brent had to drive in order to arrive at 3:29 p.m. given the wind-speed and the miles-per-gallon-of-gasoline factors. Can 518 miles per hour be right? Or is that feet per second?

How can the velocity of a falling watermelon be a negative number? Yet again!?

Maybe you've never even been able to remember which five state capitals begin with the letter A.

You've tried at home to "compare and contrast" *(Isn't that redundant? Wouldn't comparing involve contrasting?)* Thomas Jefferson's economic theories with Ronald Reagan's, but you've always messed it up some. *(Don't feel too bad. I heard once that economists don't all agree about what economic theories mean. But remember, for the test, you do have to understand what the teacher thinks the theories mean.)*

If some of this seems familiar, and assuming you're motivated to do well on the test, you will probably have the heebie-jeebies at test time. Now let's say you're congenitally deaf. The test is going to be given to you in your second or third language, a language you don't often use and one you've never heard—English. Many of the details of the language—like the meaning distinctions of the prefixes *un* and *sub*—are not commonplace to you. *(These nuances are not comprehended by many people whose native tongue is English.)* For you the lecture is in one language, ASL, and the test is in another, English. For the deaf student whose academic life contains the above scenario, the test-taking situation seems like a foreign battlefield instead of a comfortable environment for demonstrating learned knowledge or skill. Deaf students who are assessed or graded by tools like quizzes, tests, reports in front of the class, or project presentations are working within special circumstances. Below I present some of these situations and my suggestions to the instructor for alleviating these predicaments.

The ASL Lectures and The English Tests

THE PREDICAMENT: Lectures are presented in ASL. Tests are in English. Deaf students may be less familiar with technical terms, specialized vocabulary, esoteric phrases, and similar structures than the hearing students. When interpreting, I always fingerspell such expressions the first time they're used. Then I create a sign for each one and use those signs thereafter. Sometimes the students themselves will offer signs, and I will use them. I have specialized signs for algebraic and trigonometric functions, for concepts in psychology, and for periods and eras studied in history classes. Many deaf students tell me they conceptualize and learn by mentally using the signs instead of thinking in English. Their understanding is then tested in English.

THE SOLUTION: The interpreter may be required to change terms or entire test questions into ASL. NOTE: The interpreter is not an unfair advantage to the deaf student but rather a fair equalizer. Instructors and hearing students should feel comfortable that professional interpreters will maintain the integrity of the test question. We will not indicate to the deaf student which is a correct or incorrect answer. Only twice in my interpreting career have deaf students asked me how to answer an exam question. Both times I refused to respond.

The Eyes Are the Eyes and Ears

THE PREDICAMENT: Unlike hearing students, deaf students cannot read or write *and* listen at the same time. Sometimes teachers dictate lists, sentences, or paragraphs that the students are to write. Other times instructors will hand out tests and then orally have the students correct typos or other mistakes on the exams. If the corrections are numerous and the teacher speaks quickly, the deaf student will probably have a problem keeping up. When quizzes are finished, teachers occasionally give their classes the correct answers. Instructors usually do this orally and in an overwhelming scurry. "1 is C, 2 is H, 3 is False, 4 is President Harding, 5 is 1918, 6 is The Industrial Revolution, 7 is B or D, 8 is . . . ." Numbers 8, 9, and the others don't matter. The deaf student and the interpreter have given up.

THE SOLUTION: Instructors could write the information on the board or give a written copy to the deaf student. When teachers have not been willing to write the information or speak slowly, I, as an interpreter, have actually gone to the deaf student's desk and done the writing and correcting myself. However if I have more than one deaf student in the class, this won't work. Clearly the best solution is the teacher's providing the communication in writing.

The Talkative Teacher

THE PREDICAMENT: From time to time I have encountered loquacious teachers who talk to the class all during the test. These yackety-yaks (*with all due respect, of course*) rarely have anything to say relevant to the test. Once in a while they will say something important like a homework assignment or that there will be no class next Tuesday.

THE SOLUTION: Teachers should organize whatever they want to say to the class and say it before the test begins. Then they should be quiet. If a teacher rambles during an exam, I will inform the deaf student that the teacher is continuing to talk. Then I will give the student the choice, "Do you want me to interpret everything or just tell you if he says something I think you need to know?" Always, always the student chooses the latter!

I once was interpreting in an oil painting art class. All semester the teacher talked to the students while they were looking at and working with their canvases. Because this situation presented a course-long problem for the deaf student, I discussed my I'll-decide-what's-important solution with the teacher. She happily agreed that would be fine. Thereafter she spent more individual instruction time with her deaf student.

The Oral Report

THE PREDICAMENT: *Oral* reports for hearing students are usually *manual* reports for deaf students. Presentations students make to the class—project descriptions, speeches, explanations of research papers, and so forth—are definitely a special circumstance for deaf students who communicate in sign language. The interpreter will convert the signs into voiced English. (*I always change positions from facing the class to sitting in the front row facing the signer.*) The voicing should accurately reflect the content and mood of the presenter. A potential problem pops up when one realizes that the English word choice is largely the prerogative of the interpreter. For example, the deaf student could sign five signs that the interpreter could accurately voice as: "The patient became ill and then died." or "The patient contracted the disease and eventually expired." or "The patient got sick and croaked."

Another plight that presentations by deaf students bring is interpreter error. Interpreters—even the best ones—will occasionally misspeak or vocally stumble having then to backtrack and make corrections.

THE SOLUTION: The deaf student could furnish the interpreter with a written rough draft of the presentation. Seeing key concepts, English word preferences, and proper nouns ahead of time would give the interpreter a big advantage. (*Some may say* *that a skilled professional interpreter shouldn't need such a crutch. As for me, I'll use any assistance available to do the best job I can. Pride causes stumbling. Acknowledgment of weakness is a strength.*)

Instructors, when evaluating deaf student presentations, should keep in mind that the student may be somewhat more or somewhat less articulate than the interpreter. Remember also that if the interpreter misspoke or stumbled, it doesn't necessarily mean the deaf student did. I do not advocate lower grading standards for deaf students. I do suggest that these special circumstances should be considered.

The Essay Tests

THE PREDICAMENT: Eeeek! It's an essay test! If that's the screech from the hearing students, the apprehension in some deaf students at the thought of writing a few paragraphs is *Eeeek!* times two. Again the deaf student's fret is having to precisely and correctly express knowledge in a language not his primary language.

ASL is a language with its own syntax, grammar, word order, vocabulary, slang, and idioms. Many times when people whose primary language is ASL express themselves in written English, the "accent" is apparent. For example, the English articles *a, an*, and *the* do not exist in ASL. (*Although ASL has ways to express the meanings the English articles convey.*) Consequently, some deaf students have difficulty knowing where to use *the* in the sentence. Irregular English verbs are another problem as ASL has no irregular verbs. Additionally, essay questions or instructions usually contain words the precise meanings of which must be particularly understood.

THE SOLUTION: I don't have a solution for assisting students, hearing or deaf, to express themselves in writing during an essay test. Perhaps just knowing reasons some deaf students are less proficient in the subtleties of English usage than others will bring understanding to instructors.

I do have a suggestion for interpreters. We can help deaf students know more exactly what is expected of them on the essay test if we ourselves more clearly understand some word definitions to more accurately interpret those words. I am grateful to Pam Barr, counselor and Applied Psychology instructor at Saddleback College, for providing to me the following list of test words and their meanings. INTERPRETERS AND STUDENTS: Learn these!

An Enumeration of Essay Test Verbs

1. **COMPARE** — Bring out points of similarity and differences

2. **CONTRAST** — Show differences when placed side by side

3. **CRITICIZE** — Give your judgment; approve or disapprove; give good and bad points

4. **DEFINE** — Give the meaning; explain the nature of something

5. **DESCRIBE** — Tell about, give a word picture that characterizes, not just the name or label

6. **DIAGRAM**—Make a drawing, chart or graph and, usually, add labels; if possible add a brief description

7. **DISCUSS**—Examine, analyze carefully, give reasons pro and con; be complete and give details

8. **ENUMERATE**—Give a numbered list; briefly discuss each item

9. **EVALUATE**—Cite both advantages and disadvantages; include appraisal of authorities and your own opinion

10. **EXPLAIN**—Make clear, interpret, make plain

11. **IDENTIFY**—Name, label, classify, or characterize

12. **ILLUSTRATE**—Make clear by stories, examples, or diagrams

13. **INTERPRET**—Translate, give examples, give your opinion

14. **JUSTIFY**—Prove your point, give your argument; discuss bad and good points, and conclude with good

15. **LIST**—Write a numbered list

16. **OUTLINE**—Give the main ideas in organized arrangement; use headings and subheadings to give a well-ordered list

17. **PROVE**—Establish that something is true by citing facts or giving logical reasons

18. **RELATE**—Stress associations or connections between ideas

19. **REVIEW**—Analyze a subject critically

20. **STATE**—Present the main points briefly

21. **SUMMARIZE**—Give the main points concisely

22. **TRACE**—Give a description of progress in a definite order; follow sequential development

Knowing the denotations of the above terms will help the interpreter clearly convey to the deaf student what is required by an essay question. After having done that, we interpreters should sit back and allow the challenge of the test to do its work and the students to do theirs.

The Orally Administered Tests

THE PREDICAMENT: Orally administered objective tests can present a problem. The usual types of questions asked are true-false, fill-in-the-blank, short-answer, or multiple-choice. If the instructor speaks too quickly or doesn't pause between a question and the repetition of that question, the deaf student may miss some important parts of the communication. Sometimes the repetition of a question is worded differently than the original question. Suppose, for example, the teacher asks a short-answer question, "Neonates are born with certain adaptive responses. What are two of them?" The deaf student looks at his paper and thinks for a moment as does everyone else. Then the teacher immediately says, "Newborns are born with some helpful reflexes. Name two." The deaf student will miss the benefits of the second phrasing. If the interpreter can get the deaf student's attention and sign the teacher's second utterance, making clear the precise rephrasing, all is well. While the deaf student is writing *rooting* and *blinking*, the teacher begins his next question. "Who is most identified with cognitive-development theory: Erikson, Freud, Piaget, or Bron-fenbrenner?" The interpreter mentally loads this question and the four options and waits for the deaf student to look up.

THE SOLUTION: The instructor can stop this difficulty by slowing down and being aware of the deaf student's eyes. Please remember, a deaf person is hard pressed to write and listen at the same time. For interpreters to mentally load lists of proper names, technical words, or numbers is laborious, and his probability of error increases.

The Pop Quizzes

THE PREDICAMENT: Pop quizzes at the end of a lecture give no time for the deaf student to review notes in English. Deaf students usually have a fellow student volunteer to take notes on special no-carbon-required copy paper that is then given to the deaf student at the end of class. The deaf student is disadvantaged in that he has not seen the highlights of the lecture in written English as the other students have by looking at their own notes.

THE SOLUTION: If the instructor gives everyone a short time to review between the lecture and the quiz, the playing field will be made level for the deaf student.

The Fine-Drawn Distinctions

THE PREDICAMENT: Subtle meaning differences of similar words such as *continual* and *continuous* can be troublesome if correctly responding to the test requires knowing the difference. If we interpreters know the fine-drawn distinction of English words, we can sign the concepts correctly. The problem, though, is twofold: (1) we interpreters don't always know the distinctions and (2) again, the deaf student is receiving the teaching in ASL and is being tested in English.

THE SOLUTION: If the instructor emphasizes the meaning distinctions in the lecture, both the student and the interpreter will learn at the same time. The emphasis will give opportunity for the interpreter to fingerspell the words involved and appropriate different signs to each.

The Answer Races

THE PREDICAMENT: Exercises, during which the teacher asks the class a question and the student first to raise a hand is called on to answer, are irksome for the deaf. These are races he will never win because of the interpreter's lag time.

THE SOLUTION: All would be made fair if the questions were presented in written form and revealed to all students at the same time. Two ways to do this would be: (1) by flash cards distributed to everyone to be turned question side up on a signal from the teacher or (2) by the use of an overhead projector.

The Interpreter Outs

THE PREDICAMENT: Instructors sometimes believe that the interpreter's presence for the test is unnecessary, and the instructors tell the interpreter that. If the interpreter asks the deaf student, "Do you need me here for the test?", the student may cordially answer that he does not. (*I never ask deaf clients if they* need *me with them. I ask them if they* want *me with them. The preference for the word choice should be obvious, I think.*) The situation becomes bothersome when one realizes that the presence of an interpreter is a comfort for many, if not most, deaf people. Hearing people all know that if unexpected expressive or receptive communication should become necessary during an exam, they are ready for that. A deaf person should have the same ease of mind.

THE SOLUTION: Interpreters should show up for all class meetings including tests. (*I always bring something to read!*) I kindly thank the teacher for the offer and tell him that I am required to be there. Many of my deaf student clients tell me they will be fine without me. All have later told me they were glad I decided to be there.

The Instructor Outs

THE PREDICAMENT: Sometimes, when I am working as an interpreter during a test, the teacher will whisper to me that he is stepping out of the room for a while and would I please watch the class. I don't monitor during exams because doing so would violate my role with the students. (*See Chapter 5.*)

THE SOLUTION: I simply respond to the teacher, "I'm not allowed to monitor tests." (*Actually, I'm the one who disallows myself. No one senior to me at the colleges has ever discussed the topic with me.*) My position on this issue has always been readily accepted by the instructors. Some select to leave the room anyway. In their absence I have never seen an occurrence of cheating, although I have witnessed cheating with the teacher present.

The Spelling Tests

THE PREDICAMENT: Spelling tests!! Happily spelling tests are rare in college, but they do take place in English classes designed to build vocabulary. The problem is that in order for me, the interpreter, to convey a precise English word to a deaf student I have to fingerspell the word. When I've done that the student knows what to write. One time I interpreted (*fingerspelled*) the entire spelling test. The teacher wasn't alert to the problem. (*Is it my role to tell him?*) The deaf student (*and I*) aced the test!

THE SOLUTION: The solution? I honestly don't know. If the word to be spelled is a sign's gloss word (*an English word most commonly associated with a particular sign*), expressing that sign might work. But there's no guarantee for the deaf student that the gloss word is the exact word he is to write. Additionally one sign expressed alone without a syntactical context will not convey to the student whether the adverbial, adjectival, or another form of the word is desired. An English word like *rambunctious*, which is not a gloss word, would present another problem. While the concept of rambunctiousness can certainly be expressed in ASL, the student could correctly interpret the signing as *boisterous, hyperactive, rowdy, obstreperous,* or a host of other English words.

The interpreter could mouth the word, but all of the shortcomings and pitfalls that plague lipreading would come into play.

Interpreters often employ a technique known as Total Communication that essentially means do whatever is necessary to get the meaning across. Total Communication classically involves signs, fingerspelling, mouthing, facial expressions, gesturing, and maybe even writing. Total Communication won't work with spellings tests either because many of its aspects would violate the integrity of the test. Obviously educational interpreting is not an exact science. An interpreter's smock is not a lab coat. (*Interpreters' smocks are uglier.*) I'll wait for someone who is more inventive than I to devise a solution to the spelling test conundrum.

Tests and quizzes and other graded classroom activities raise their own set of difficulties for a deaf student, his interpreter, and his teacher. Fortunately, most of these wrinkles can be ironed out with a little attention to the deaf student's special circumstances and by making a few minor adjustments in the classroom.

"The dangers of knowledge are not to be compared with the dangers of ignorance. Man is more likely to miss his way in darkness than in twilight; in twilight than in full sun."

—Whately

"The light intrudes and the darkness cowers into itself."

—Jim Brewington

Chapter 5

If You Help Me Do My Job, I Can Help You Do Yours

(The Interpreter's Role in The Classroom)

The interpreter has a clear-cut and well-defined duty in the classroom, but different interpreters approach the role with different amounts of fervor and zeal. At the high-energy end of the continuum is the take-charge, set-it-up, tell-em-how-it's-done, do-it-right, confident professional. On the other extreme is a flat-line personality sitting meekly, facing the class in the only chair available that sits in a place decided by the teacher or the deaf student, an interpreter who makes finger-in-the-wind decisions and who flaps and flops a droning sign language with a low-to-medium energy level—and he is completely voice activated, of course.

The arrogant inflexibility of the first guy described above is as uncongenial and displeasing in interpreters as it is in teachers. The flaccid-willed, weak-as-water, existence of the second guy is ineffectual, and besides, his presence contributes greatly to the grey banality that cascades from the cornucopia of commonness in far too many classrooms.

Proper and palatable interpreter protocol resides between the behaviors of the two bunglers I just characterized. We interpreters assume a set of definite responsibilities in the classroom or any other place we are working. The success of the educational process for the hearing-impaired student depends, in part, on the teacher's skill to articulate his teachings, his awareness of the specialized techniques necessary for teaching the deaf, and his willingness to cooperate with the interpreter and the student. The student must be enthusiastic to learn and participate, and the interpreter must be a strong yet flexible bridge joining the deaf student with any English speaking person or device.

The gears of this educational mechanism are best lubricated with the oil of submissive cooperation. If each person regards the other participants as more important than himself, we have a setup for success. (*This rubric for the classroom is a principle for life that, when applied, provides a setup for success in any relationship.*)

The solid and great majority of the teachers under whom I have studied, and with whom I have had the privilege to work as an interpreter, have been passionate in their profession, humble in their personality, and cooperative in their participation. However, contrastingly, found in some classrooms is a rare but occasional character, the negative exception.

This Narcissistic egomaniac is inflated with the pride of his own academic accomplishments. He peacocks before *his* class as General Patton strutted before his troops. He is clad only in the cris-cross plaid of his own insecurities. He demeans the students and perhaps the interpreter and speaks condescendingly to them. He scoffs at incorrect responses to his questions and inhibits student participation, which he demands. He unflinchingly declares, defends, and emphasizes his own self-made, two-step hierarchy in *his* classroom: He is captain of this ship and everyone else isn't. (*Doesn't the classroom, the whole school, exist for the students, and aren't we, who are on staff, there to serve them?*) He requires on-time exact obedience to his assignments. He demands respect, but he commands none. He expects cheating on his exams. He doesn't monitor his tests; he patrols. He cracks the scourge at anyone fighting drowsiness not considering that his class meets after lunch in a warm room and that his lectures are the phenobarbital of public speaking. He is humorless. This führer operates alone; he cooperates with no one.

One faculty despot and I encountered each other in *his* classroom once, and then I saw to it that we encountered each other outside of *his* classroom. (*Seems as though we duked it out on the playground. Well, sort of.*) Here's the story.

My home phone rang at about 4:30 in the afternoon one day in midspring. It was Ginny Harris, the saint in the Special Services office at Saddleback college who oversees interpreter scheduling among other things. She needed an interpreter to substitute in a class beginning at seven o'clock that evening, because the regular interpreter had become ill. The regular interpreter was a good friend of mine; in addition, we had worked together many times in several different settings. We admired each other's interpreting skill, and we have often noticed and fondly teased each other about the vast differences in our signing styles.

Ginny gave me the necessary information for that night's job. The building and room number were familiar to me. That room in the Science and Math building had tiered rows of seats like the auditorium lecture halls of many large universities. A chalkboard spanned the width of the entire front wall except for comfortable left and right margins of blank wall space on either side providing an out-of-the-way area with a visually neutral background for the interpreter. The room was without windows, so I didn't have to worry about signing in front of a light source, a cardinal sin. The teacher's space between the first row of seats and the front wall was ample. It was a nice room. I had worked in it many times.

The subject was prealgebra math. I had interpreted in several math and algebra classes, and I'm comfortable working in those areas of study. (*Everything okay so far.*)

The teacher's name was unknown to me, and his reputation, good or bad, had not reached me. But I was a substitute in midsemester, so he was used to having an interpreter nearby. (*That should be fine.*)

The student, too, was new to me. Though I had met her once, I had never interpreted for her. I had no idea what method of communication she preferred. (*But no big deal.*) Usually agreement on this important issue is reached quickly during the early moments of our meeting each other. However, many signs used by college interpreters are not universal, common, familiar, or understood by all — signs for some places such as Rwanda or Lubbock, signs for various Presidents of the United States (*my sign for Teddy Roosevelt, the sign for bear with initialized R's because of his connection with the Teddy Bear, is very different from my sign for Franklin D. Roosevelt, the sign for wheelchair with initialized R's*), or signs for concepts technical to a subject such as *factor, foil, function,* and *asymptote,* which are used in algebra classes. All such signs need to be established and agreed upon by both student and interpreter. Mutual acceptance of a sign usually happens on the fly as the lecture is in process, and almost always, all this takes place without missing a beat of the lecture.

Okay, well there's the setup, and here's what happened. I showed up outside the classroom about ten minutes early. In about five minutes the student arrived with a hearing friend. She and her buddy were having a conversation that I chose not to interrupt. A couple of minutes passed, and she headed toward the classroom door. She glanced at me. I signed to her that I was the interpreter and that my name was Jim. We exchanged niceties; she mentioned to me she remembered seeing me in the Special Services office, and we walked into the room. During our brief exchange, I noticed two or three SEE signs and that her sign order was very English, a clue to the signing style she might prefer.

Emily took a seat in the front row a third of the way from the outside aisle. Spotting the interpreter's chair near the corner, I walked toward it. My peripheral vision—exercised to improve, to become expanded, sharp, and useful—caught her signing to me that the teacher *wants* the interpreter directly in front of Emily. The tone of her signing let me know that the instructor was emphatic about his wants. My antenna and my guard went up at the same time. The chair placement was acceptable but not optimal. For one thing I was sitting between the student and a portion of the chalkboard that, if the teacher decided to use, would be blocked by my head, upper body and signing arms and hands. The second problem was that I was too close to the student, about 3½ feet away from her. I like a minimum distance of five feet. Communication received by sign language can be most clearly and easily understood if the perception of the signer and his range of motion is included in one easily viewed picture. If the interpreter and the student are in each other's faces, a disadvantage exists that is cumbersome and exhausting for both. (*I wondered why the regular interpreter didn't raise Cain about this. I made a mental memo to ask her, as I had never known her to allow anyone to inhibit her with regard to her doing what she believes is professionally best.*) For a moment I repeated my own thought that as a substitute I would work from this position one session, but I would never endure a whole semester from this perch.

The room was ready. The pupils were in their places, papers and pencils out and books opened. The overhead lights were on and their rheostat was adjusted. The board tray was stocked with chalk and the interpreter was poised. The wall clock's minute hand touched the 12 of seven o'clock. At the rear of the room the entrance door swung open, seemingly of its own accord, and therefrom presented Himself, His Royal Highness, The Majesty of Math, The Sovereign Prince of Pre-Algebra!

The chatting in the room hushed—I sensed from fear and not respect. Now, not only was my antenna up, but my radar was rotating and radiating. I surveyed the faces of the students to assess the situation. All the faces had gone deadpan.

I glanced back at His Knowledgeness. He had paused on the top tier of the room for no discernable reason except perhaps to survey his range and domain.

His robes were not regal. His cords and Kmart plaid short-sleeved shirt with collar stiffs mumbled a fashion statement in casual frump. He shuffled and dragged one sandaled foot after the other to the front of his realm.

His first words were to me. Omitting cordialities, he demanded, "Move your chair forward. I need room to pace." He gestured in the direction of Emily with a commanding hand that could have appropriately held a scepter.

I looked unbelievingly across the already short distance to Emily's eyes. She sent me a facial expression that said, "Let's just live with it; it's not worth the hassle."

With reticence I acquiesced. The roll call had begun. My left hand awkwardly grabbed the seat of the chair as my right hand furiously fingerspelled the names of the class roll at rapid-fire speed. All the while the chair and I were hopping obediently forward.

The roll call finished without ado. A review of the homework problems was launched with fury. Previously all of the math teachers I had interpreted used an overhead projector or the writing board to display the math problems, equations, matrices, and so forth. That's nice for interpreters for a couple of reasons: first, the deaf student has two visual opportunities to grasp the topic—the board and the signing; second, because the instructor is usually speaking what he writes as he writes it, the speech rate is slowed to something manageable for the interpreter.

Mr. Math didn't use the board for the homework review. The solutions to his division of fractions problems heaved from his mouth to splatter on the students at an explosive rate. He put forth the numbers and terms so fast he could not pronounce them properly. Some of his sentences—if they could be called that—weren't completed, so that piled on the interpreter the burden of using cloze skills. (*I talk about cloze skills in Chapter 3, and yes, it's spelled with a z.*)

When he paused (*I wondered if he was oxygen depleted.*), I used the moment to sign to the deaf student. "Are you understanding me okay, or would you like me to sign like your regular interpreter?" I signed the last half of that thought imitating the style of the other interpreter. Emily laughed without sound, and I smiled.

By this time, the teacher had resumed, and I was one sentence behind. Catching up, I heard him say, "Are you translating everything I'm saying exactly?" (*Is he speaking directly to me? Whom else? Is he con-*

cerned for me and my ability to keep up? His tone seems accusing.)

Presuming he was concerned for me, but not really sure, I nodded yes and exercised my professional prerogative not to become personally involved in any dialog.

Then he spewed, "I said, 'Are you translating everything I'm saying exactly?'." This time there was no mistaking his tone. These words were coated in bile.

I was stunned but not nonplused. The slow burn of retaliation was ignited in me. All of the students were looking at me, waiting. Several thoughts quickly popped up for consideration. (*I'm an interpreter, not a translator. I don't translate anything, exactly or otherwise. I should say "no."*) (*What pushed his emotional button? Why this tug-of-war? Doesn't he realize he and I are pulling on the same end of the educational rope?*) (*My self-control and professional dignity and courtesy will prevail!*) "Yes, I am."

"Well," he asserted, "she's laughing, and I didn't tell a joke." (*You've probably never told a joke.*)

Because I had signed everything he had spoken, Emily was looking at me with embarrassment on her face. Her eyes, looking like saucers, were filled with astonishment. (*I was astounded too. No teacher since Mr. Watts in the ninth grade had ever spoken to me like this.*)

He paused, waiting, I guessed, for an answer to his implied question. I made my move. I turned my head to the right, but eye contact with him was not available.

(*Was he cowering behind me?*) "If you would like to have a professional conversation about my responsibilities in this room, I will be happy to have that with you after your teaching." (*There, I like the way that came out, assertive and cordial. Surely he'll agree and we can get all this straightened out after clash—I mean after class.*)

"I just want to teach a class here without interruptions or distractions. I have a class to teach here; I just want to go on and teach my class here." (*Well then, why don't you just get on with it?*)

I wanted out of the active role situation as quickly as possible. He didn't speak to me directly again. I sat professionally neutral and dutifully interpreted the remainder of the session.

An hour and a half later he proclaimed that class was over, resolutely closed a couple of math texts that he tucked under his right arm, and he headed for the door. I was nonexistent.

Scrambling to catch up with him I spotted him outside and approached with purpose in my stride. With a voice that left no mistake I intended to control this conversation, I asked, "Just exactly what was it that upset you in there?"

"I know you weren't translating exactly what I was saying." His accusing tone let me know once again he believed he caught me committing a rebellious crime. (*That did it. It's time that his arrogance with ignorance met a match: my anger with information.*)

I decided to reply with firm, very firm kindness never letting go of dignity. "You're right. I wasn't translating anything. I'm not a translator; I'm an interpreter. And I was interpreting everything you were saying, plus I was communicating information to the student, information necessary for me to do my job. It's understandable and perfectly fine with me that you are unaware of the technical aspects of my profession. (*I heard my voice become slightly louder, so I told myself to keep the volume control in check.*) And if you want to display your ignorance in front of your class, that's up to you, but you redressed me in there. I won't tolerate that. Don't *ever* censure me in public again."

He glared at me. (*I guess he expected nothing less than full-blown homage.*) "Who [sic] do you work for?" His retort was vitriolic.

"I work *with* Special Services, and if you want me to put our two deans together on this one, it'll be my pleasure." (*That should take care of his attempt to intimidate me.*)

He fired the next salvo. "What you were doing was distractive, and I would have stopped any student causing a distraction."

"What I was doing was necessary, and I was being as unobtrusive as I could be." (*I presumed he had experienced some envy that more of the students had their eyes on me than on him. This is a common occurrence with interpreters' work. The students' curiosity with the signing and the signer wanes and their eyes return to the teacher in about 10 or 15 minutes usually. Of course, every class has one or two students who remain intrigued with us all semester, and if swear words or sex words are used,* **everyone** *turns to us in drill team unison to see the signs. More about this subject can be found in Chapter 9.*)

I pressed on by explaining to him that I had received a phone call asking me to sub in his class only late that afternoon, that I had never worked with the student before, that I needed to establish some ground rules and blah, blah, blah. (*I was now ready to conclude this educational effort, but I could sense some of my own steam blowing off, hissing out around the gasket of my cool demeanor.*) "I have as much responsibility and right to perform my professional duties in the classroom as you do. Usually, I receive cooperation from the instructor, not opposition, but in the face of opposition, I will do what I must within the margins of ethics and dignity to be the best interpreter for my clients that I can be. And that's true even when one of my clients is supplying the opposition."

He apparently regarded the last point of my speech as a barb pointed at him, for he said, "Let's just pray we never have to see each other again." (*Pray?! The word caught me off guard. He didn't seem like a man of prayer to me. Maybe I had become the force to drive this pride-basted soul to the throne room of God. Hallelujah. Either that, or he was just using a borrowed, unfamiliar vernacularism!*) He turned on his heel and darted at a clipping pace away from me.

From 15 yards and increasing, I blurted with softness in my voice, "That's not my desire. I just don't want you to chew me out in public again."

He stopped, turned around, glared into my eyes for about five long seconds, turned back around, and disappeared around a corner into a hallway maze containing classroom doors and more classroom doors. I haven't seen him again.

Focused as I was on our conversation, I had not noticed that several of his students had been standing at a distance observing all of this. They approached me now and told me they were glad someone finally stood up to him, that there was no excuse for the way he had treated me, and that they had considered saying something to him about his haughty attitude, but they were afraid their grades would suffer. (*Wow, I thought I may have overreacted, but I guess I didn't.*) Not wanting to become embroiled in a playground gossip session, I spoke no unkind words about the instructor, thanked the students for their encouraging words, said goodnight, and walked to my car.

The next day I reported the incident to my supervisor who listened with acceptance and offered to handle the matter anyway I liked. I told her to let it die unless we hear any repercussions from the math department. She promised to inform me if anything was reported. We never heard another word about it.

I have just related to you an incident of extremes. As an interpreter I had never experienced such hostility as that in a working situation, and I have not since. I suppose my fellow interpreters, after reading the above exchange, will react variously. Some will flinch that I dared to respond in such an outspoken way. Others may applaud my gumption. Wherever you land on this spectrum of opinion, please be encouraged in knowing that at least one interpreter believes we have implied authority in the classroom, and elsewhere, authority to require the interpreting environment, insofar as is practical, be established and maintained in a way so as to promote and enhance clear communication comfortably received by all clients.

Please know that the indignity suffered was not mine, and my ego was not the source of the outrage. Criticizing a working interpreter is much like jerking on the harness of someone's seeing-eye dog or kicking someone's crutches out of reach. Such a display of insensitivity to a person's need is so immense in immorality and so crude in self-centeredness that the Bible commands against it and those with common decency recoil at the sight of it. (*"Do not curse the deaf or put a stumbling block in front of the blind . . . ."*

—*Leviticus 19:14*)

I was ticked. Ticked with dignity can be an admirable attitude for interpreters to hold in reserve. Other approaches should be tried first, but anger for righteous reasons has a place on my menu of moral responses. *Moral?* Yes. I view our duty to work for conditions conducive to clear communication a moral duty. Morals supersede ethics. (**You can read more of my thoughts on this concept in Chapter 8.**)

Here is a list of suggestions for ensuring the interpreting environment is the most productive it can be. I address the suggestions to interpreters who should be responsible for such things, but instructors and students too can well benefit from knowing this information. The order of the list reflects no particular value of priority.

1. Let there be sound. I have interpreted for college students in classrooms, laboratories, dark rooms (*That's a rip-snorting delight!*), theaters, and gymnasiums, swimming pools and day care centers, on golf courses and construction sights, with counselors, financial aid administrators, and friends. All of these situations have peripheral sounds—sounds that are not the priority focus. I'm talking about jets and helicopters, thunder, cars, sirens, sneezes, coughs, burps, hammering, wind, screaming, giggling, crying, laughter, susurration, nose blowing, beepers, cell phones, public address announcements, crashing books, pencil sharpeners, printing presses, murmurings, side comments, quiet swearing, loud swearing, whispering, cooking food, radios, televisions, air-conditioners, crackling fire, lawn mowers, and on and on and on.

The hearing student receives all or most of this audible input for good or bad. The hearing student knows from listening to a person's voice if it's masculine, effeminate, baritone or high-pitched, nasal or lilting, lisping or melodic, or if it has an accent—from Germany or the Bronx, from the South, or from Chicago.

Most peripheral sounds I leave alone. I omit them from my interpreting. I ignore them for a couple of reasons: (1) The deaf people I've worked with have told me they don't need to know about them—they don't use the information anyway, and (2) interpreting all that stuff becomes visual noise, a distraction.

The exception to my own rule is made if the peripheral sounds become a focus. If the burp is so loud that people react to it, I explain that. If people turn around to look at the back windows because of the sound of a sudden downpour, if people startle because a book has belly flopped on the floor, I make sure the deaf people are clued in. If I can't hear a comment from a student in the room because people are talking, I make that known to the deaf. Oh yeah, one more exception: I convey some noises or sounds such as a squeaking door hinge, just because I feel like it. It's my professional freedom. My guidelines are flexible, and they all leave room for judgment or impulse. (*The fine line between judgment and impulse is probably a factor of time.*)

Accents are a different horse, and so are other vocal mannerisms. By vocal mannerisms, I mean speech impediments, unusual voice tone, pitch, volume, or other qualities. Now I admit I'm not sure that knowing a voice is nasal or raspy or guttural is important to a deaf person unless someone responds to that voice trait, but some regional dialect information does carry connotations for some people.

A dialectic blight that has infested Southern California and, I'm told, other regions of the United States, is the upward inflection of syllables that end phrases, clauses, and complete sentences. People often use such an inflection at the end of question sentences to indicate inquiry. Because this trendy (*Oh please, let it be trendy.*) habit ostensibly originated in the San Fernando Valley, many people call it "Valley talk." Some local dialecticians refer to it as "up talk."

For a reason unknown to me, most of the people who use up talk in my area, it seems, are females in their teens and twenties. They are stereotyped as chatty airheads tending to be hyper and giddy with an underdeveloped grip on their emotions. This characterization, true or untrue, fair or unfair, exists as a cultural by-product in the hearing world. The deaf, who may be informed of this stereotype, cannot recognize its presence, however, because this colorful weirdness is conveyed by voice only.

So what's the interpreter supposed to do? The bilingual-bicultural method of interpreting compels or allows me to inform the deaf clients of the unusual intonation without telling them what to conclude about it. This is tricky business. In real-life interpreting, how much I explain or convey to the deaf depends on how busy I am. I can't fall behind with the bilingual part of my job, that is, with interpreting the content of Miss Valley Girl's talk. But the way she sounds is important to mention because of the connotations associated with the dialect and because other listeners may react to her speaking style.

I usually deal with this situation by signing that she talks like a Valley girl. Most of my deaf clients have understood this. If I get a quizzical facial expression, I will explain, time permitting, that she talks like some young people from the San Fernando Valley and then let the deaf draw their own conclusion from the content.

Men who have effeminate speech and women who have masculine speech present a similar situation. Once, after I signed to a student that the male speaker has effeminate speech, the student asked me if the speaker was gay. "How would I know?" I told him. "Do you want me to ask him?"

As an interpreter, I impart whatever nonverbal sounds I perceive with my ears if I determine (*guess!*) they are significant or will become significant, and that's it. Conclusions and judgments from me about the sounds are taboo.

2. Let there be light. The darker the room the better for slide shows, overhead presentation, films, and video tape showings, and the like — unless you're deaf. The deaf need to see the interpreter *and* the projected image. By the way, the closer the interpreter and the projected image are to each other, the easier is the task of seeing both at the same time. If it's audio-visual aids time and my student is instantly plunged into a black gulf of a room, I let the teacher know immediately, but in a gentle, polite way, that I can't operate in the dark. No matter how politely and humbly I mention that we need *some* light, the class invariably laughs at the obvious oversight. When some light is turned on, some enlightenment is turned on as well. Oh please, **LET THERE BE LIGHT.**

Photography teachers and some graphic arts teachers require students to gather in dark rooms to listen to a lecture or two about film developing or to watch (*!*) a demonstration of the equipment. All of my guidelines about the interpreter's standing near the teacher or the demonstration go out the nonexistent window. I drag the deaf student as close to the overhead red light as I can, and I interpret with as much of the red light falling on me as possible. Sometimes I need to nudge a few hearing students out of the way. "Excuse me, excuse us please, pardon me, may I get over here please, thank you, excuse me . . . ."

If, during this process of my seeking light, the teacher has begun the lecture, I will probably ask him to hold on for a minute until I'm situated. "Okay, thank you, I'm ready."

While I will assert myself to ensure the interpreting environment is the best it can be, I don't tamper with or make comments (*out loud*) about the content, clarity, or accuracy of the lecture itself. (*But the temptation to do so is strong enough to give me empathy for drug addicts.*)

Suppose this: the photography teacher grabs some bottle and holds it under the dim red hue above a sink containing three or four flat dip pans. As the deaf student squints to see my signs, the instructor hastens to say, "Now what we need to do first is you need to get some of this (*long chemical name that needs to be fingerspelled*) that comes under different brand names such as (*he names a few brands, and I stab at spelling them*) that you can buy at (*he names three or four suppliers' names I've never heard before*) and what you do is you take and pour about this much of this bottle into this pan here." Every *this* requires visual contact with something: "this much," "this bottle," "this pan." Of course, with the interpreter's lag time, by the time I've signed "this much" or "this bottle" and the deaf student looks away from me to search for "this" and I wait for him to look back, the lecture has moved on. (*I'm doomed. The deaf student is doomed. We're all doomed.*) But I don't mess with the content of the lecture. (*I just pray for light.*)

3. Blazing the visual path. Some nonlecture situations such as class critiques of graphic arts projects or construction site work or discussing a visual aid showing the moons of Saturn or a review of the safety rules for a gym machine designed to strengthen one's gastrocnemius muscles all require some adjusting of the interpreting environment.

I stand as close to the object—three dimensional design project, model of the solar system, drywall patch job—as I can. The idea is for the deaf student to have a clear, unobstructed, visual path through the crowd of gathered students to the object of attention, the speaker, and the interpreter.

Often, indeed probably always, a speaker who is talking about an object that is in front of him will point and use the words *this, that,* and *over there.* Because all such words require the deaf student to shift visual focus from the interpreter to the speaker's pointing finger, a close proximity of object, speaker, and interpreter is a good thing. Because I believe I'm the only one in the room to have considered this concept, I will take the initiative to thrash out the path. Usually, gesturing to the students with a swimming breast stroke motion to part the sea is sufficient, but sometimes I need to give a short explanation in English. I'm comfortable in being as politely assertive as is necessary to get the job done.

Here's one last observation about these gather-around-the-thing situations. Probably because of some informality perceived, the students tend to chat and offer forth corny, hackneyed, one-liner attempts at humor during these times. Some of these attempts at humor succeed. I will interpret as many of these asides that I can without forgetting the main speaker, but if five or six people are spewing their comments at the same time, I find myself picking and choosing what to interpret. That's fine until someone's witticism actually works and people laugh. (*Why is it always the difficult-to-interpret word-plays that get a reaction? "Your bowl-of-fruit painting is overly purple. Don't you think you kind of went bananas with the plums?"*)

4. Oh Come On, Gimme a Break: Interpreters need breaks. Students need breaks. Teachers need breaks, but especially interpreters need breaks. Many hearing students and a couple of instructors have asked me if my hands and arms get tired. No, they really don't. It's my brain that gets mushy. The interpreter is undoubtedly the only person in the classroom who listens to every word. In making that statement, I include the teacher. The interpreter is the only person in the classroom who processes in two languages every concept, phrase, clause, fragment, and run-on.

This processing becomes mentally exhausting—and in short order. The research articles I have read (*Yep, people have actually conducted empirical studies of interpreters' performances.*) all conclude that an interpreter's error rate increases shortly after 20 minutes of work. The error rate conversely decreases sharply after a 10- to 15-minute break. Well, unless two interpreters are working the same class, a 10-minute break every 20 minutes doesn't make practical sense in a classroom situation. On the other hand, a 10-minute break every 50 minutes makes enormous sense for everyone.

Why, then, is it that so many instructors, people with gobs of formal education and classroom experience on both sides of the lectern, can't get a grip on this simple concept? If all of the educational and psychological research on learning concepts and processes, on attention span, on information retention, and so forth were all discarded, wouldn't common sense and personal experience let one know that a person's brain and butt get numb at approximately the same time?

Yet more than just a few teachers I have interpreted refuse to give breaks. Most often their explanation is that they have too much material to present in too short a time. Apparently they believe the educational process is concerned with the teacher's presenting of material instead of the student's learning of it. These teachers serve 10 courses of their meal at every sitting surely believing the students are greedy and gluttonous, willing to gorge themselves at an academic Thanksgiving feast. (*Get real. What an egotistical naivete!*)

Another explanation I've heard for withholding breaks is in, say a three-hour class, "We'll go straight through, put both breaks at the end, and we'll all go home early." Sometimes the majority of students actually vote for this. (*I guess they too have discarded wisdom for freedom.*)

Both of these no-break justifications are paltry and unworthy of consideration to me, the interpreter. When my brain (*both left and right hemispheres working overtime, you know*) becomes pasty and pulpy, my interpreting skills—accuracy, clarity, and the rest of

90

it—are going to take a break whether the teacher likes it or not.

Two solutions to this problem are available.

(1) During the summer sessions when courses are compressed and lectures are lengthened or for sessions any time that are longer than two hours, the Special Services department graciously and wisely assigns two interpreters to each class. We spell each other every 20 minutes. This team system works beautifully. I have read someone's opinion that a frequent change of interpreters rattles the deaf student. No deaf student I've served has ever given a hint of verification to this notion.

(2) The other solution to the no-break attitude is to insist on a break. My first approach to the instructor to explain my need for short intermissions is gentle—almost sheepish, humble—almost meek, friendly, kind, and cordial with a smile—almost endearing. This attitude is admirable and is almost always unsuccessful. My next approach, a modulated key change I make immediately and smoothly during the same conversation, is a cordial double assertion that my professional skills require a short rest every 50 minutes or so and that I will be taking a break whether the rest of the class does or not. (*When will these teachers realize that the rest of the class will take a mental break, voluntarily or involuntarily, anyway?*)

This assertion of mine usually brings slightly more intense and prolonged eye contact from the instructor, but my genuinely friendly, smiling face generally dissuades them to think again about the break situation. If the teacher's hesitation continues, I will say furthermore that during my break one of *your* students, who wants to learn, will be receiving none of the information being provided.

Only one exception breaks a perfect success record for this approach. He taught construction techniques, framing, drywall installing, house building—that type of thing. After my why-I-need-a-break speech, he agreed to give into 10 minutes every hour of his four-hour class. But he didn't do it!

At the next class meeting, after two hours of a non-stop sleeper on the care and use of a gazillion power tools, I limply signed to the deaf student, his eyes crossed and at half-mast, that I was going to break now. I got up and matter-of-factly, without an attitude, walked out of the room. Moments later the class filed out of the room; they were given a break. I returned to the teacher and reexplained that I will not interpret for two hours plus without rest and that I hoped my walking out was not disruptive. He let me know that it was and that he had a lot of material to teach. Further, with a gruff laugh, he admitted he had forgotten about me . . . hawrrr, hawrrr, hawrrr. (*I got the feeling he wanted to sock me in the arm and invite me to join him for an evening to drink beer, shoot pool, talk construction, and look at women.*) "Ahwrrr, that's okay," I gruffed, "I'll just let you know every time I need a break by walking out and taking one."

"Haawrrr," his belly was bouncing. "That'll be good."

After every 50 minutes of lecture for the rest of the semester I walked out of the room for a break, and the class shortly followed having been granted a break of their own. My classroom friendship with the teacher was a good one, testosterone-driven and peppered with frequent exchanges of guffaws. As my path was directed, we worked together the following semester too. He lectured and demonstrated tools and techniques, and I interpreted and decided when the breaks would be. (*And I learned a lot about construction tools and techniques!*)

For though I am not under the direction of the instructors, I have placed myself in service to them that I may effect a relationship. With historians I have adapted to the ways of historians that I may win their favor. To the anthropologists, though I am not an anthropologist, I express my genuine interest in anthropology for the sake of relationship. To the sensitive, I become sensitive. To the gruff, I become gruff. To the technical, I become technical. To the artful, I become artful. I have learned to express the part of me (*which is sincere and genuine to be sure*) that relates best with my fellow for the sake of kindness and friendship. Success doesn't depend on the use of rules or methods, but rather in working well with people. About breaks, be firm; about people, be flexible.

5. Please don't muzzle my hands. Please give the deaf student and me the freedom to converse with each other anytime we want. The purely professional interpreting organizations will probably flinch at the idea of an interpreter and a deaf student chatting in a working classroom setting. In the real world, snippets of conversation occur often. I see three levels of appropriateness here.

(1) Some interpreter-student exchanges are very important; they add or ensure clarity to the communication process. For example, some deaf people cause one of their cheeks to twitch near their nose or they raise one eyebrow. Either action means "I understand." Sometimes signs are created or provided, disputed, explained, corrected, or rejected. Establishing sign clarity is usually a very quick process, and occasionally agreement on the use of a new sign — or an old one — involves humor. Because they are created in haste, some suggestions for signs, either by the interpreter or the student, are funny. (*Once a student laughed out loud when I showed him my sign for Calvin Coolidge, the "C" hand shape moving across my mouth with my lips pressed tightly together because Silent Cal was taciturn and tight-lipped.*) Such moments may cause us to smile when smiling is inappropriate to the lecture or teaching. Teachers: please understand that your presentation is being interpreted completely, that the student and I are working things out to ensure clarity, and that having a good time is not counterproductive to learning, nor is it unethical. I suppose you, the teacher, need to trust the professionalism of the interpreter remembering that while my bonding seems to be — like my eye contact — with the student, I am loyal to my duty of presenting clearly everything you are saying.

(2) The second category of proffered discourse between the student and the interpreter is probably inappropriate, but I acknowledge it and accept it anyway. This talk, at least with me, always originates with the deaf student. It usually consists of a quick one-liner. Here are some examples:

"May I borrow a dollar for the break, just until I see you again?"

"Did you go to Deaf Awareness Day at Disneyland last weekend?"

"Before I arrived, did the teacher say anything about the quiz on Thursday?"

"Wow! Look at all the buttons on that calculator."

All such questions or comments can be given a quick "yes" or "no," and that's that. If the deaf student wants me to elaborate, — "What did you do at Disneyland? How long did you stay?" — I tell him we can talk later.

I discourage this kind of private talk between student and interpreter, but I don't wig out when it happens. I'm tolerant of it. I was taught in interpreting school to ignore this signed chat or (*Here's some really brilliant guidance.*) voice it. If you're an interpreter and you want to see a deaf student come out of his skin, try voicing one of these private moments. Next step, pray for an abundance of mercy.

Teachers: I suggest that *you* ignore this momentary distraction between deaf student and interpreter. I'll deal with it, and it'll be over soon. Hearing students whisper among themselves. That's tolerated to a point. Please don't pounce on a deaf student faster than you would a hearing student. I ask for your patience, and besides, because you are probably dealing with unfamiliar territory when you enter the arena of deafness, the risk factor of embarrassing yourself is sky high.

(3) The third type of deaf student-interpreter communication is radically inappropriate, and I won't participate in it. I'm talking about any attempt at prolonged off-topic conversation. If, for example, the deaf student signs, "This is boring, wow! Next weekend David, you know David, we're going to Las Vegas. Have you been there since they built the big pyramid-shaped hotel?"

My response: "Not now, later. I'm busy interpreting here." This message comes with a facial expression that conveys that I'm serious but not angry. When deaf students want to gab during class, I become unsettled. These conversations are conspicuous. The teachers usually mention them either during or after class. I don't want to be personally involved in a confrontation between the teacher and the student.

Other comments from student clients to which I don't respond are those that give or ask for opinions. Examples:

"This teacher's a bozo. He should join a circus."

"No way, I don't think big lips are sensuous. Do you?"

"That girl right there, she's cute, right? But she talks too much."

"This class doesn't help critical thinking. It's stupid."

I may give a quick and subtle eyebrow raise to let the student know I understood what he said, but, after that, my face couldn't be more blank. I have worked at developing a facial expression that says nothing, and the minority of deaf students who say this kind of thing to me understand that no response is a response. They know I won't participate.

I won't participate for a couple of reasons.

(1) I'm not here to teach or express any opinions, to agree or disagree with anyone. (*Although sometimes the temptation to become involved is close to overwhelming.*) I'm certainly not going to act at cross purposes to the instructor.

(2) Every person in the room is potentially a client. The moment anyone speaks and I interpret what they've said, they have become my client. My sense of loyalty to my clients will not allow me to express or agree with opinions about them, especially negative opinions. The moral principle of regarding other people as more important than myself supersedes any ethical rule in this regard.

Therefore I request of my hearing clients, especially teachers, that you trust my professionalism, well-intended heart, and common sense when the deaf and I are signing to each other. No kind consideration or purity of purpose will be breached.

6. **Please don't muzzle my mouth.** Here I address the deaf students with the converse of the above concept. I don't sign all my private conversations just because someone deaf is nearby. Sometimes before or after class or during breaks I have conversations that I do not sign. The instructor or hearing students may come up to me to talk. Usually, these chats are small talk and do not mention the deaf student. Often,

hearing people are curious about how long I've been an interpreter, where I learned to sign, if my arms get tired (*No, it's my brain that gets numb.*), if I learn a lot being in all the classes (*Sometimes, but usually, I'm too busy working with language units to assimilate much information.*), if I do this full time (*No.*), etc. Oftentimes, I hear that they learned the manual alphabet in elementary school and that they always wanted to learn to sign. (*I encourage them to do that.*) Occasionally students recognize me from other classes and want to say hi. All of this is individual, one-on-one, shooting the breeze, and I feel no obligation to sign it. Most, if not all, deaf students I know are fine with that, and you should be too.

Let me step out of context for a moment to explain that in social situations—e.g.: parties, theater intermissions, meeting breaks, etc.—when both deaf people and interpreters are present and mingling, correct etiquette seems unclear or, at least, inconsistent. For example, here are two true stories.

I was working as an interpreter in a beginning ASL class. The instructor was deaf. The class ended, and a couple of hearing students lingered to chat with me. As the instructor was packing up getting ready to go, another deaf instructor came into the room to talk to the teacher. They used ASL, no voices. The beginning students were enraptured with the fast-paced ASL and asked me what they were saying. I voiced the conversation for a moment or two. One of the deaf instructors caught a glimpse of me and asked if I was voicing them. I told him yes, and he became incensed. His hands snapped at me telling me never to do that—that their conversation was private. It didn't seem to matter that if they had been hearing people using voices we could have heard every word they were saying and listening to them would not be considered rude at all.

The second true story: I was with another interpreter on the lawn of a church with a predominantly deaf congregation. Because it was before the service, people were arriving and gathering in couples and groups of three or four to chat. ASL was fast if not furious. My friend and I were talking to each other, voice only, when a small, seemingly frail, deaf lady trotted up with resolute direction to tell us with staccato fingers that we were to sign here, that there were many deaf people here and that using our voices only (*for our private conversation!*) was rude.

Perhaps these two incidents have some social differences sufficient to justify what seems to me a confusing ethic, but both experiences serve to illustrate an etiquette expected by many deaf people that I have found in most social situations where deaf people and hearing people are present together. IF YOU'RE HEARING AND YOU CAN SIGN BUT YOU DON'T—THAT'S RUDE. IF YOU VOICE AN ASL CONVERSATION TO A HEARING PERSON WHO DOESN'T UNDERSTAND ASL—THAT'S RUDE. If you're hearing, please take this observation from my experience bank and deposit it in your own so you can avoid offending deaf people who agree with the etiquette. If you're deaf, please consider that hearing people have as much right to a private conversation as the deaf. As an interpreter, I may have a private, voice-only, conversation with another hearing person when you are in the same room. Your being offended by this, is, in my opinion, inappropriate.

The final example of behavior I will personally strive to eliminate wherever I go is a conduct and demeanor oftentimes attached, indeed draped over, the interpreter. We interpreters have for a long time been told we are conduits of communication much like a telephone. We are merely a device, neutral of personality ourselves. We are to convey only the feelings, emphasis, and the expressions of "the expresser of the source language." Consequently, many interpreters arrive at work clad with all of the human demeanor of a beige desk phone. (*Not me, man. If this isn't going to be gratifying, agreeable, congenial, and amiable, count me out. I am not just a human signing machine. I'm a guy with traits and idiosyncrasies, and it's about time the hearing and the deaf calm down and allow me to be real. I'm a person who's part of what's going on here.*) Who decided that stoical is ethical? Interpreters, I understand this concept may be radically opposed to your training and practice. For the moment, take some relief that maybe it's okay for our face to be more than a blob of silly putty plopped at-the-ready for the always-in-control "expresser of the source language" to knead at his whim and caprice. More of this notion, this view, is found in the following chapters.

Situational Interpreting Difficulties

English-ASL educational interpreting is an inexact discipline. The interpreting courses I took were good ones, but they didn't—and I'm sure couldn't—prepare me for all of the bizarre interpreting challenges I've confronted.

This chapter is about the interpreter's role in the classroom. The classroom, however, is not always a classroom. I have interpreted college courses while standing on a ladder to a loft that was under construction, while standing in a photography darkroom, and at pool side for water polo practice. I've worked while running alongside a cross-country track team and strolling on the campus from exotic tree to novel shrub with a biology class. I've dodged balls in a racquetball court while trying to discern the coach's instructions as they echoed off the walls. I've prompted in ASL from the wings of theater stages during rehearsals and performances. I've turned a hand on volleyball courts, in weight-lifting gyms, in computer labs, in team transport vans, at baseball and basketball games, and in a reading lab. I've rolled up my sleeves to walk backwards in front of groups touring the campus, the library, the newspaper offices, and the radio station. The ceramics kiln, the dissecting table, the graduation ceremony, the telephone registration procedure, and the around-the-room, around-the-world map tour have all presented odd moments. The above is the short list of offbeat predicaments that have arisen.

I have no rules and barely any guidelines for dealing with all of these scenes. I know that I have a job to do, and I'll do it however I have to. I am assertive enough to relocate people in settings (*all by request, of course*) including the deaf students, the instructor, and the hearing students.

I don't hesitate to become mobile myself. In classrooms I sit on a padded stool that has a back. (*I set one up in each classroom in which I will be working at the beginning of each semester. I put on each stool a flyer that says, "Interpreter's Chair. Please Do Not Remove. Thank you, Special Services."*) These stools are on wheels and they have an adjustment lever that allows the seat to be raised or lowered. The rolling stools let me glide back and forth in front of the board so the deaf student's eyes can see the teacher's writing and my signing at the same time. The idea of a floating interpreter glissading around the front of the room is unorthodox and requires a little getting used to by some instructors. I am very sensitive of their location, and I make sure I stay out of their way so as not to restrict their freedom. Most teachers adjust quickly, and every single deaf student for whom I've interpreted has thanked me for being mobile. (*This practice is called* **shadowing.**)

But be aware, please, I don't feel chained to the stool. I will follow teachers around the room as they point to maps, art projects, and the like. I stand next to the television during video tape showings. I place myself near students giving group presentations.

Interpreters in the educational setting are facilitators of communication. That role is always complex and sometimes difficult. Interpreting is a job requiring much training and skill and oftentimes innovation and a willingness to break the rules. (*There are no rules, but most of us interpreters have been taught there are.*)

Carl Sandburg wrote that Abraham Lincoln was "a man of steel and velvet, hard as rock and soft as drifting fog." Similarly, interpreters must walk the fence of being assertive yet not demanding, professional yet human, involved yet neutral, expressive and mobile yet inconspicuous, and firm for the sake of our clients yet cordial and accepting for the sake of all. We beseech the cooperation of the instructors, and the students, both deaf and hearing. As we all seek to understand the roles we have in the classroom, we will realize our common educational goal—to learn, to grow, to develop, and to mature.

"The thing to do is to supply light and not heat."

—Woodrow Wilson

"Through love to light! O wonderful the way that leads from darkness to the perfect day!"

—R.W. Gilder

Chapter 6

Getting to Know You

(The Interpreter-Teacher Relationship)

Relationships are life. They are the bedrock foundation and the pinnacle of our souls. Relationships are the whole shebang of our existence, our raison d'être. This concept is known to be true by psychologists, sociologists, medical professionals, business experts, religious leaders, psychotherapists, laborers, bartenders, educators, taxi drivers, politicians, engineers, animal experts, lawyers, students, teachers, and sign language interpreters. All living people who love another person can testify to their own vivacity and joy. Creatures plodding through their years without giving or receiving, without interactive friendships, are the walking dead. People without affiliations or kinships are often ignored (*which intensifies their state*), or they are encouraged to seek help.

Given these two groups of people, those who relate (*the vivacious and joyous*) and those who don't relate

(They would have to describe their own feelings—but they wouldn't.), I choose to be in the first group. I, therefore, reject any suggestion that I, as a sign language interpreter, should work in a classroom and not interact or reciprocate with the teacher or the students.

Quickly, while some interpreters are gasping, believing this bolt from the blue has blind-sided their longstanding value of detachment, let me note the worth of discretion. Knowing how much one can interact in which circumstances, at what time, and in which tone or mood depends on the nature of the relationship. The nature of the relationship between, say the teacher and the interpreter, needs to be defined. (*I believe the continual process of defining is helpful in any relationship.*) When we know a little bit about each other and our role in each other's lives, we can more easily exercise discretion in our relationship.

I always try to contact the teacher to whom I've been assigned before our first class, just for the purpose of discussing our roles in the classroom. Preferably this meeting is face-to-face. Oftentimes, it is not, because of the teacher's unavailability. Interpreters and Teachers: I urge you to make yourselves available for a meeting before your first class. Teachers: please don't dismiss the need for chatting with the interpreter just because you have worked with an interpreter before. Interpreters have individual preferences, needs, and quirks. You are establishing a relationship with a person. Each relationship is unique. Allow an hour, so you're not rushed. Ask of each other all the questions that occur to you. Personal questions appropriate to a first meeting are good too.

Here is a partial list of some questions you may want to ask. (*The answers to these questions, and more, are found in this book.*)

Questions the TEACHER may want to ask the INTERPRETER:

(1) Do I need to talk slowly? Does it matter how fast I talk?

(2) Do you have to sit in the front? Aren't you a distraction for the other students?

(3) Can you keep me posted on how the deaf student is doing?

(4) What do we do about oral reports?

(5) What about discussion groups?

(6) Do you explain things the deaf student doesn't understand?

(7) Are you going on our field trips with us?

(8) How will the deaf student ask questions, and is it okay for me to call on the deaf student?

(9) Can't the deaf student just read my lips?

(10) What can I do to help?

Interpreters: If you are so fortunate as to be asked question #10 above, resist the temptation to teach a four-unit course in Advanced Interpreting. (*Chapter 9 may be helpful.*) On a couple of occasions, I have overwhelmed teachers with verbose suggestions. Both times I experienced cooperation shutdown. Remember, most deafness concepts are new thoughts for hearing people. Information overload is uncomfortable, and the purpose here is to create a comfortable, cooperative friendship.

Questions the INTERPRETER may want to ask the TEACHER:

(1) Do you write much on the board?

(2) Do you use video tapes or overheads?

(3) May I have a copy of the course syllabus and class handouts now?

(4) Do you have a glossary of technical terms you will be using?

(5) Are your tests written or orally administered? Are they objective or essay?

(6) Do you conduct class discussions?

(7) Could you please notify Special Services if you need to cancel a class meeting?

(8) Have you ever had a deaf student before?

(9) If yes, how was that experience for you?

(10) What can I do to help?

I have listed below some of the definition I would like to provide instructors regarding our professional interpreter-teacher relationship.

(1) I am present to facilitate communication between the hearing and the deaf. I try to be sensitive to everyone's needs, but I am not in submission to every-

one's wishes. I am available to serve anyone who needs my interpreter services, but I don't like to be ordered around and told what to do. I will reflect (*and sometimes feel*) the tone and mood of the moment— e.g.: levity, anger, bitterness, sadness, or even urgency—but I don't want to be the target of a teacher's or student's frustration aggression.

(2) I don't monitor tests when the teacher is out of the room. If I see a student cheating, I don't report it. I've heard this topic of interpreter's reporting cheaters discussed in some of the interpreter workshops I've attended. Some argue interpreters should report violations of school policy because we are staffed by the college. Besides being the grandfather of all non sequiturs, this reasoning fails to recognize that our reporting would put us in an adversarial association with those whom we serve. Reporting affronts our neutral position and does all sorts of damage to the comfortable environment we seek for easy, open communication. Besides, test monitoring isn't our job.

(3) Here are a few other things teachers have asked me to do. I've responded with polite no's to all of them, though I may be somewhat qualified for any of them. While I'm working as an interpreter:

(a) I don't teach ASL, English grammar, Biblical studies, U.S. history, or any other topic. (*Actually, I have occasionally spoken to classes when asked, but there must be another interpreter present to work when I'm addressing the class.*)

(b) I don't serve as a subject for a demonstration of the Heimlich maneuver. (*This one caught me by surprise once in an English As A Second Language class—go figure! Before I knew what was happening, the 60-something year old teacher had slithered up behind me when I was trying to remember how to fingerspell Heimlich. Instantly, her hands were locked at my chest. My arms were constricted under hers. Did Heimlich do it this way? My sternum was receiving rhythmic thrusts from her combined fists. My lungs were forcibly emptied, and my eyes were white and bulging like a pug's.)* Please don't use me for a demo dummy.

(c) I don't run errands

(d) I don't operate VCR's (*Well, usually I don't.*)

(e) I don't discuss the deaf student's private life. (*One teacher asked me once to explain to the class just exactly what the deaf student could and could not hear. In the first place, how in the world would I know? In the second place, how in the world would the deaf student know just exactly what he cannot hear?*)

(f) I don't express opinions, political, religious, or otherwise. (*I am continually surprised how often I'm asked my opinions while I'm working. Perhaps the growing number of gray hairs on my head bespeaks of wisdom. I almost always have an opinion, and I am almost always tempted to offer it if asked, but I don't. A working interpreter has no business opining. And that's my opinion!*)

These things I listed are examples of guidelines; they're not rules. Wisdom mandates sound judgment and flexibility. So does friendship.

I will plug in an overhead projector, catch the light switch, pick up a dropped book, or do whatever I can as long as my work is not interrupted or disturbed. Sometimes I will even supply information. If, for example, the teacher is talking about Uganda, but has momentarily forgotten the name of Uganda's capital, and I happen to remember it's Kampala, I'll tell him. Of course, in doing this I'm dipping my toe into the waters of unorthodoxy. I'm careful that none of the students are trying to volunteer the information. I make sure the teacher is really, really wanting to know the elusive name. I have to be confident, without doubt, that I am right. Even then, I hesitate, but, if all conditions are satisfied, I will stick my toe in and say, "Kampala." How do I know I won't offend the teacher? Because I know the teacher. We've established a relationship.

To me a good teacher-interpreter working relationship is one of mutual respect for each other's professional knowledge, purposes, and methods. We begin and depart each class meeting with friendly, first name niceties. Usually the teacher introduces me to the class on the first day. Occasionally, a teacher will gratefully acknowledge me during the semester. I always appreciate that. (*Once a teacher said, "Let's watch Jim work." Then he spoke a series of nouns: tree, zebra, circus, moon, etc. He wanted to see the signs. I didn't mind that. Everyone is entitled to a little fun sometimes, and the students probably benefitted from the break.*) I enjoy any recognition that is cordial or encouraging or helpful to the class. Teachers have used me as an illustration when discussing certain topics such as eye-hand coordination, peripheral vision, stimulus-response behavior, linguistics, etc. I don't like, however, any reference that makes a spectacle of ASL or me or the deaf student. (*Another "teacher" played the say-the-word-and-watch-the-sign game with me, only this time with a list of sexually explicit words and swear words. In my mind that crossed the line of mutual respect. Although each word the teacher spoke had a sign, I fingerspelled them all, to the teacher's expressed disappointment. I never understood the teacher's purpose here. If I'm going to do nothing, I want to really do nothing instead of doing something that amounts to nothing.*)

Unfortunately the interpreter must relate and endure the occasional teacher who brings into the classroom the bitterness, anger, frustration, or the crass indecency of his heart. For example, in a few of the classes where I have worked, the teachers seem to be running on a fuel of animosity toward the students, as though the bitter bile of banality has been dripping into their gullet for so long its level has risen to overflowing and sometimes spews into the ears of all nearby. Nearly anything can stimulate an outburst from these pent-up pedagogues, but most often a student's inattention opens the valve. (*I wonder if these gifts to instructional education ever considered the reason the students are heedless and unmindful, passing notes, talking, and even sleeping is because the presentation is less than spellbinding. Once, in an American history class, I was signing on and on, and, at the same time, thinking, " I'll bet this teacher has been reading these foxed, yellowed lecture notes since President Wilson actually did sign into law the Espionage Act in June of 1917. `Unless one had a theory about the nature of governments, (should I sign this the way he's droning it?) it was not clear how the Espionage Act would be*

112

used. But its double-talk concealed a singleness of purpose.') The dull knife saws and saws again without penetrating; the dull teacher does the same. Teachers: if the students are not transfixed by you or your subject or both, perhaps it's time to freshen up the act a little bit. Surely when the people who pay to listen to you are gazing attentively at you, the frustration of futility will fade away.

I have high regard and respect for 99 percent of the teachers with whom I have worked. *(Many of the teachers at Saddleback College are expert in their subjects far beyond the required standards, are wonderfully devoted to their students and profession, are innovative and fresh in their presentations, and their skills parallel or surpass the skills of their colleagues at well-known universities.)* Most of the remaining 1 percent would not have been a problem had it not been for the gap in the teacher's information regarding my role as an interpreter and, I confess, my testy, petulant, frustrated reaction to their unfamiliarity. In other words, if the teacher and I had known each other a little more, we would have been fine.

The critical element in the teacher-interpreter relationship is kindness. Being kind is much more than being cordial although cordiality is included of course. Kindness is fervently providing that which is needed. The benevolence involved in kindness requires our being focused on the other person in order to sense his needs. Then, we must respond to the needs we perceive. That's the behavior of kindness. The heart of kindness is genuine concern for the success of the other person, either personal or professional. It's a genial benefaction that produces a relationship that is symbiotic and not co-dependent. Healthy kindness brings fulfillment and a happy outcome to work in the classroom and to life outside of it.

My fellow interpreters: I charge you to be the first to reach out in kindness.

My fellow teachers: I charge you to be the first to reach out in kindness. Surely with such mutual, aggressive graciousness we will be professionals worthy of our students' emulation.

> ## *"The brightest blaze of intelligence is of incalculably less value than the smallest spark of charity."*
>
> **—W. Nivens**

"Learning, the destroyer of arrogance, begets arrogance in fools; even as light, that illumines the eye, makes owls blind."

—**Franklin Edgerton**

Chapter 7

Are You His? Do You Go With Him Everywhere?

(The Interpreter-Deaf Student Relationship)

No, as an interpreter I don't belong to the deaf student even though the student may refer to me as "my interpreter." Interpreters at the college level are assigned to classes, usually for the semester or term, not to the student. While we do not live with and stay attached to a deaf person, interpreters have an affiliation with the deaf student that is more complex than may at first be realized. This chapter unravels the intricacies and reveals the subtle — and sometimes elusive — details of that association.

"I would never, never ask an interpreter to loan me money," Doug signed to me near the end of our first class day together. "That would be like asking to borrow money from a professor. But my pockets are empty, and well — if I could maybe borrow a dollar for a coke, just until Wednesday, that would be wow. If you give me two dollars, I'll get a coke for you." Many deaf students really never would ask their interpreter for a small loan or a ride to work or for any other personal favor, but many would and do.

The interpreter-deaf student relationship is a professional one with some secondary characteristics of a personal relationship. Most deaf college students, like the hearing students, are serious about their education and their classes. They study diligently and want to earn good grades. They are accustomed to working with and relating to interpreters. Probably all deaf students recognize and appreciate the training, skill, and hard work of a talented interpreter. Every educational interpreter I have known is likewise serious about doing a good job in the classroom, a good job of facilitating communication between the deaf and the hearing.

Such a clear purpose for being there, and a sincere desire for doing well, provide a strong base for a good professional relationship between the deaf student and the interpreter. The relationship however always seems to carry a personal aspect to it. Hours and hours of face-to-face communication create many opportunities for feelings to be expressed. Students often react to what is said in classes, and interpreters *sometimes* do. Two people who watch each other's personal reactions to situations day after day will become acquainted with one another on a personal level. Intimacy develops when personal feelings are exchanged. The relationship is still professional, but it takes on another nature, an additional component. It's human; it's personal; and it's okay. A hypostatic union of two natures, professional and personal, in one relationship is normal and enjoyable. Fighting or ignoring the personal feature of a professional relationship is aberrant and stilted. It creates a cold gap between two people. I believe that gap, that aloofness, is a detriment to learning, and it puts a damper on any kind of fun or good time too.

How much individual interaction between the interpreter and the deaf student is appropriate? What's okay and what isn't when it comes to the interpreter's helping the deaf student inside or outside of the classroom? How personal, advisory, or chummy can an interpreter be and still be professional? These questions are difficult to ponder and impossible to answer without guidelines. I've never seen any rules about all this. Rules would be to rigid anyway. I work better with more wiggle room.

A system of ethics might help answer the questions above, but I have never seen a system of ethics pertaining to the interpreter-deaf student relationship. The current written ethics for the interpreting professionals are, for the most part, inattentive to the educational setting. The ethics I *have* seen seem more concerned with good and bad behavior than with moral duty and obligation. Written professional codes of ethics tend to restrict what a professional may do, while moral correctness tends to expand what a professional may do. A system of ethics without a moral base will fail.

A solid moral rock upon which to stand is mandatory for making effective, mature relationship decisions, professional or personal. I have such a solid rock foundation, though I'm still learning to stand securely there.

I intend to moralize for a moment now. Some of the following paragraphs may seem preachy. I wish only to convey ideas that will help create the most conducive learning environment for the students, including the deaf students.

Below are two of the principles helpful to me in making relationship decisions.

(1) The interpreter who has kindness in his heart is one who has a firm footing on good relationship decision making. A person who desires to help, who wants to contribute to the success of another, and who is forbearing and cordial in the process, is kind. Kindness requires providing that which is needed, not necessarily that which is desired. Kindness in the classroom requires preparing or empowering the student to work an assignment to successful completion without doing any part of the assignment for him. Kindness to the student demands assisting him without indulging him. Relationship decisions based on kindness will be correct and successful decisions universally. The personal part of the professional relationship behooves the interpreter and benefits the student.

(2) An interpreter who has a servant's heart will be well guided in his relationship with the deaf student.

We interpreters who are skilled enough to be considered professional have undergone several years of formal training and education. We attend workshops and seminars. We continually try to increase and refine our vocabularies in English and ASL. We strive to improve. Why? For what purpose? Simply, to serve others. Our gifts are to be given to others. What value is anything if it isn't used for the good of another?

Lacking humility, we could, I suppose, hold high our talents, skills, and other resources to be displayed on our individual balance sheet. Perhaps there, they would ignite envy in people. Our means could be posted in such a way that those analyzing our assets would conclude our net worth is significantly in the black. But a balance sheet's net worth is only a number until the actual asset is used for good. Our storehouse of grain is only a heap of grist until someone is fed. If one decided that one's skills are acquired for the purpose of benefitting others, then the resulting relationship is well defined.

I press this point. Most people have accepted that kindness is a good trait. But convincing some people that the main reason to get out of bed everyday is to serve others—well, that can be a tough sell. I can understand the reasoning. I grew up learning that "good ole number one" means me. For many years I believed that Jim Brewington was the most important person in my life. After all, I heard, if I don't watch out for myself, who will? Only after receiving and accepting wiser instruction did I realize that serving others is more noble that serving self. I have learned that the humble servant will be exalted by others while the self-exalted will be abased. This truth is observable in all sections of society including the college campus. Yet I occasionally encounter some teachers and some interpreters who present an academic haughtiness. Their way of looking at things, their presentation, says: "I've paid my dues. I have my degrees and my certification. I've earned my position, and you, my little student, haven't." The minority of "professionals" who strut this puffed-up posture have at least one thing in common. They all have nonexistent or lousy relationships with their students. This condescending countenance is the antidote to exhilaration, and, tragically, it is self-perpetuating. An hubristic approach precludes a caring relationship.

The antithesis to this obnoxious behavior is the getting up each day to serve the students. We teachers and interpreters should go to our classrooms with our knees bent to serve instead of with our backs arched to strut. Only then will the blessings we've received, our skills, talents, knowledge, and wisdom, become the blessings of our students. Any benefits we receive are simply by-products of our service to others. Our provision, our income, our opportunities through promotion, and the enjoyment of our work are a result of our diligence in serving faithfully. How serving our actions are is a prime consideration in determining what is the right thing to do or the wrong thing to do in the interpreter's relationship with the students.

So, what is the relationship between the interpreter and the deaf student really like? With the concepts of kindness and service laid as a foundation to help us define the interpreter-deaf student relationship, I will now let you in on some of my experiences with deaf students. I will also tell you something about the nature of the interpreter-deaf student relationship as related to me by some of my fellow interpreters.

When I was in the beginning months of my elementary schooling in Iowa, my teacher helped us all with our mitten strings and our galoshes buckles. She zipped zippers when zippers wouldn't zip. She taught us how to put away our building blocks and our nap towels. She explained the stories she read to us, and she hugged us if we cried. In the second grade my teacher resolved arguments in the classroom and brawls on the playground. Well, if she didn't resolve them at least she stopped them. My teachers were willing to loan me milk money (2¢!) if I forgot mine. They patiently guided me, their hand holding mine, through my academic assignments.

As I graduated from one grade to the next, the teachers' assistance with personal needs became less and less until sometime in late junior high school (*now in Texas*), I noticed that the teacher only taught. Most of my instructors at Texas Tech University and the University of Iowa didn't bother to learn my name, and some, I'm sure, never noticed me. What a drastic difference from kindergarten!

My interpreter friends who work at various levels in the educational process tell me the services they provide their deaf students run the gamut from help with personal hygiene needs in the lower grades to advice with organizational skills in the higher grades. Interpreting remains the primary role for the interpreter, but it is rarely the sole function.

As with the teachers in grades K through 12, where the amount of personal, nonacademic assistance is abundant in the lower grades and where it dwindles in the upper grades, so it is with the interpreters' services. By the time the deaf student is seated in his first college class, he is accustomed to school, homework, projects, tests, lectures, and interpreters. The students may need help finding the buildings on the campus, but who doesn't? (*Special Services at our college provides a tour as part of the orientation process.*) Deaf students, like most other students, need some help adjusting to the differences between high school and college, i.e., the increased study time demand, the faster-moving lectures, the greater dependence on time-management skills. A demand for self-discipline and mature judgements is sudden and stark.

Exactly how much an interpreter should assist with the deaf student's adjustment to college is impossible for me to know generally. I make case-by-case decisions about doing things for students beyond interpreting. I will do almost anything to help with the educational process stopping short of taking over the teacher's job. Time permitting, I will clarify concepts if I detect confusion, but I won't explain a concept again from A to Z. Instead, I encourage the student to ask the instructor a question. I won't fill in a student who is late to class with details of an assignment given or a future quiz already discussed, but I will summarize what has taken place so the student knows to ask for particulars himself. I may make suggestions about study skills or organization skills, but I won't tutor the student. I will direct the student to watch the board work or an overhead presentation instead of watching me if I think that's advisable, but I don't ever insist that he looks at me. I know some interpreters who demand that the deaf student look at them, but I don't. Sometimes deaf students want to pass notes to other students or sign to other deaf students, to doodle on their paper or glaze over and take a mental trip someplace. Hearing students are usually allowed to be mentally elsewhere without being nagged back to reality. Why not the deaf? The instructor may intervene and demand attention, but I don't. I believe doing so is outside of my role. (*If the instructor asks me to please make sure the deaf student pays attention, I politely remind the teacher that I will interpret whatever he says.*) So there are some of my dos and don'ts in the classroom. Generally, I will do anything I can to help the educational process, focusing primarily, of course, on facilitating communication. I don't offer assistance if doing so would eliminate or lessen an academic challenge necessary for growth. I make my daily situation-by-situation decisions based on a desire to serve with kindness.

Other aspects of the interpreter-deaf student relationship are presented topic by topic below.

What do I know about the deaf student?

Routinely teachers and hearing students ask me questions about the deaf student. Students ask me how he's doing in the class, how did he become deaf, does he like horticulture, and does he hear loud noises. Teachers ask me where he is if he's late to class, how he's doing in his other classes, if he's understanding everything, and what's causing his bad mood. They ask me about his family and where he went to high school. They ask me about his organizational skills and if he eats lunch alone. My standard answer to the inquiries is, "I'm not sure. Why don't you ask him?"

Everyone must think I am a treasury of knowledge, that I have the intimate inside lowdown on my students. Well, sometimes I do, and most of the time I don't. At times the deaf student will confide parts of his academic and personal lives to an interpreter he trusts. The basis of the trust is in place from the beginning of the relationship. The deaf person knows that the interpreter is supposed to keep his mouth shut about anything learned in interpreting situations. That ethic is usually generalized to include conversations with the deaf student inside or outside of the interpreting situation. (*I'm not sure such a generalization is written in any set of ethics or is merely justifiably concluded.*) So, at times, the deaf student will tell me bunches about his life in general and in detail.

A few years ago I would *never* have asked a student questions about himself. If he wanted to show me his graded test, I would look. I would not have asked him to show me. I was taught that to ask about his family, his background, or his deafness was an inappropriate professional malfeasance, a first-rate, stepping-over-the-line taboo. Now, I'm not so sure. I'm more bold to question but never interrogate, to inquire but never require an answer, to seek but never prowl. I believe my sincere concern evidences kindness and enhances the relationship. Furthermore the information given to me helps me to better understand the student, all of which facilitates communication.

Trust is at the core of the deaf student-interpreter relationship (*and any other relationship*). The trust cannot be merely assumed. It must be demonstrated and earned. As an interpreter, I'm part of the team of teachers, tutors, counselors, Special Services experts, librarians, coaches, and others involved with the education of the deaf student, but I won't discuss him with any other team member without his, the deaf student's, permission. I allow him to decide how much I interact with the other team members. Usually the deaf student gives me his approval. However many times the deaf student regards his relationship with me as inviolable. He chatted with me or confided in me not expecting me to ask his consent to divulge his privacy. He hopes I won't talk about him. I always, always honor his desire. My fellow team members have, without exception, graciously accepted my resolve to be still if I choose.

In summary:

(1) If you want to know something about the deaf student, ask *him*.

(2) Deaf students: think twice about allowing us interpreters to share our perspectives with educators who are interested in your success. Our views may be enlightening to hearing educators and therefore beneficial to you. Assess our hearts and motives. Then make a well-considered decision.

(3) Interpreters: when in doubt, keep your hands folded and your mouths shut.

Anecdotes

Below is the report of some incidents I've experienced while interpreting. They are true to the facts except for the peoples' names. My responses to the situations should demonstrate the principles I've iter-

ated and should help make clear my sense of the interpreter and deaf student relationship.

Rick The Impetuous

Eighteen years old and the oldest of four siblings,
Rick had responsibilities at home and college that
seemed overwhelming to him. His home, headed by a
loving mother, had been a home without a father since
just before Rick's eighth birthday when his dad aban-
doned them. Mom worked hard to provide for the
family's needs, but as the kids grew older she felt clob-
bered by the economy in Orange County and
overmastered by the needs of the children. Rick was
expected to fill in the gap by working a full-time job in
addition to his 12 units of college courses. Rick was
handsome, athletic, friendly, frustrated, short-
tempered, and deaf. The two pleasures he asked from
life were to attend his church's youth group activities,
and to participate on one of the college's sports teams.
His church had no interpreter. He joined the cross-
country racing squad, and I was assigned to interpret
in that "class."

When I showed up in the P.E. department, the
cross-country coach told me I was welcome to stay but
I really wasn't needed. "Rick will be fine. We really
can't baby these kids, you know. They have to learn to
get along in this world," he taught me. I let him know
I thought I should stay explaining the policies of Spe-
cial Services and Rick's desire to have an interpreter.
(*I refrained from running through the ABC's of the
Americans with Disabilities Act.*) The coach said,
"Fine." I got the feeling he resented my explanation.

While the coach was cordial, attentive, and helpful to Rick, the stay-tough-grow-'em-up attitude prevailed toward Rick and, it seemed, to me and to a couple of other team members. It was obvious to me that the coach's occasional barbs were sparks landing near Rick's short fuse.

My role was to interpret the class lectures and then hang around as the team loped off over hill and horizon for their workout. The class lectures were really team meetings—pep rallies during which the coach sometimes used off-color language and then drew attention to my signing of those expressions. Rick later told me he viewed this game as a mockery of ASL and, by extension, a trivializing of his deaf culture and of his deafness itself.

Strictly speaking, I suppose, my operational purpose is to interpret—only. In an effort, though, to help keep the lid on Rick's simmering emotions, I took him to one side and told him not to let the coach get to him. "You should," I suggested, "learn from him, work hard, contribute to the team, and have fun."

"Yeah, but he doesn't know anything about deafness," Rick said with frustration in his signs.

"I know," I signed. "I'll try to make him aware."

I did chat with the coach about some aspects of deafness, but my words fell on truly deaf ears. (*This interpreter's function of acting as a cross-cultural advisor and mediator, while once taboo, is now gaining some acceptance in the interpreting profession. THANK GOD!*)

I rode in the team van to the first competitive meet. It was across the county. I interpreted the fast and wild conversations during the trip, allowing Rick to be included in the jokes and the chatter and the fun. After we arrived at the meet site, I interpreted the directions for warm-ups, the starting time, the rules for the race, and the team members' friendly talk back and forth. Nothing was said about my interpreting the course direction. The coach said to them that the route of the race would be obvious to them as they ran it, and I interpreted that information for Rick. The anxious herd of bunched-up runners behind the start line heard the starter yell a last-minute something about flags and turns along the route. Rick was somewhere in the middle of the mob. Standing in a multitude of spectators myself, I couldn't get Rick's attention to interpret information about flags and corners or anything else to him.

The starting gun fired, and the stampede thundered. Rick was with the horde as the different paces began to change the crushing pack into a line that disappeared behind a yonder hill. After about 30 minutes of their running—only God knows where—the leaders who had sprinted out ahead were seen chasing our way and losing no time about it. Near my position at the start line, a confusing fork in the course had been constructed with posts and flags and a female in a house dress (*and nothing to designate her as an official*) planted near the route's V. As the racers approached, the woman, who, with her hands in her pockets, blurted at them to bear right. Their path then veered sharply right sending them down into a gully where they disappeared from our sight, circled around, returned via the left leg of the V and ran onto the original path against the remaining, oncoming traffic! The only lid on what would have been pure pandemonium at this junction was the voice from the flower-print dress.

Rick had not shown up and was nowhere to be seen. I saw other latecomers straggle in, and then I spotted Rick, alone and distant, lagging but still enthusiastically travailing toward us. Then, I noticed still other participants behind him.

Sweaty and flush, Rick approached the V with puzzlement and panic on his face. Now bored with her job, the violets-on-cotton turned to chat with a friend. She never told Rick to bear right. (*It wouldn't have mattered anyway.*) Rick made the wrong turn.

I ducked under the ropes strung to keep the fans back, chased after Rick and, at full pace and alongside, I signed for him to turn around and take the other route. His wrong guess allowed those trailing Rick to pass him. Rick turned around and finished the race. He finished dead last.

I approached Rick who, bent over with his hands on his knees, was gasping and panting for breath. The more air he gulped the more angry he became. "Why didn't anyone tell me the right way? Why wasn't a sign posted? I can't hear what they're saying, you know. Why doesn't anyone understand that?!"

As I began to give Rick some feeble explanation (*Inwardly I sympathized with him and agreed.*), he turned on his heel and headed for the coach, now standing near his assembled team. I hurried to catch up so I could interpret what I thought would be a fiery moment.

Rick crossed his arms at his waist, grabbed the tail of his sweat-drenched tank top and pulled it off over the top of his head. In his understandable, clear speech be bellowed at the coach, "You don't understand anything about deafness! You and your team suck! I quit. I'm outta here." Rick threw his shirt at the coach hitting him in the face. Rick turned and stormed away from us.

"Rick, come back here right now," the coach barked at Rick's back.

I said quietly, "Coach, that won't work. He's deaf." (*I shared Rick's frustration about the lack of deaf awareness, but I tried not to show it. Some hearing people say and do really stupid things in the presence of deaf people.*)

"Well, what's his problem?" the coach asked me.

I explained briefly the confusion at the course's intersection, and then, without waiting for a response, I picked up the shirt, excused myself, and left to find Rick. I was miffed at Rick for his behavior. I was miffed at the coach, not for his naivete of deafness, but for his arrogance, which converted his ignorance to stupidity. I was miffed at myself for not having tried to bring more light into this abysmal darkness.

Rick was far from the crowd, alone and sobbing, when I found him. I let him know that his frustrations may be justifiable but that his behavior was not. He knew that already. (*A large percentage of counseling, correcting, and encouraging is telling people what they already know. The reiteration of truth with loving-kindness seems to aid the healing process.*)

Riding back to the college campus in the van, Rick and I ignored the conversations of the other students. Because we signed, our talk was private. Empathizing with his stresses and problems, I gave Rick kinder, acceptable options for responding to others, especially others in authority. I suggested to Rick that he apologize to the coach and that he ask the coach to reinstate him. Rick did, and the coach did.

Subsequent to the cross-country race, Rick and I attended his church's youth group meetings. I interpreted. While this work at Rick's church was without pay, it was not without benefit. Rick found friends, the path to peace, and proper ways to relate to authority. I received joy from watching Rick grow and change. I later made an opportunity to chat with the coach about deafness. He seemed receptive to learning. I like this part of my work. It's a role, a duty, that they didn't teach me in interpreting school.

Peter The Unprepared

Peter's English class began at ten o'clock in the morning, but Peter didn't. The professor was a stickler for starting precisely at 10:00 a.m. As the clock's second hand swept by the 12, her instruction commenced. In more class meetings than not, the instructor, at 10:00:00, told the students to list 15 items in some category she would name. They had 60 seconds to complete the task. The exercises were always finished at 10:02 on the outside. No mention was made of taking out a clean piece of notebook paper and a pen. These were college students. They could figure that out on their own. After a couple of frantic class starts with students scrambling in their backpacks and note-books for paper and pen, most students caught on, arrived a little early, and were ready to write at 10 o'clock sharp.

This was not a lesson quickly learned by the deaf student, lackadaisical, disorganized, tardy Peter. Shuf-fling languidly into class at 10:03 or 10:04, he missed the first two exercises completely. Old-school inter-preting would say that all of this is none of the interpreter's affair. I suggested to Peter that he pretend the class starts at 9:55, that he be seated and ready to write at 9:57 or 9:58, that he have his homework as-signment out of his notebook ready to turn in, and that his text be out and marked at today's lesson. All of these ideas seemed reasonable, if not somewhat obses-sive, to Peter except for showing up at 9:55.

"We shouldn't have to be here at 9:55 for a 10:00 class," he balked.

None of Peter's characteristics described above are stereotypical of any group of people I know including the deaf. Surely every group has individual members who are nonchalant, disarranged, and habitually latish except, I suppose, the Navy Seals and the cast of River-dance. Because Peter was burdened with idiosyncra-sies needing improvement — and he could see that — he gratefully accepted all of my suggestions except for arriving early! That idea offended the core of his soul.

Not all deaf people are unpunctual, of course. But members of the deaf community I've had experience with are characteristically casual about being on time. Some of my deaf friends have tee shirts that teach about "Deaf Standard Time," and some have nicknames in sign (*"nick" name signs*) that are variations of the sign for tardy. Not all deaf people are habitually late, but I can honestly tell you that I have never known a deaf person who is consistently early. Indeed, some of my deaf acquaintances would say that to arrive places early is a waste of time and stupid. Some loosely defined, but observable apathy about punctuality seems to thread through parts of the deaf culture. Because this trait in people makes me crazy, I've tried to change my deaf friends. I have been 100 percent unsuccessful.

Educational interpreters: I believe giving our students some suggestions regarding organizational skills and study skills is the kind thing to do and a good idea. Don't get your heart broken if only some of the help is accepted. Peter came to class on time and completed his exercises for the duration of the time he stayed enrolled in the class. He never arrived more that 30 seconds early.

Stan The Intermittent

Stan was a student in the community college system since—oh, I don't know—the beginning of the Harding administration until his graduation in the spring of 2000. Since the advent of the 1990's I interpreted a catalog full of courses for him. He dropped classes like bombers dropped bombs in World War II, in clumps. He changed his major more than once. He registered for water polo so many times he was forced to retire from the team. He played sports so hard and so well he was often too tired to attend classes or stay awake during them. (*In some classes, not all the blame for falling asleep was his.*) Stan is a bright, fun, and funny guy, yet, when he attended class — and he was not tired — he was an academic achiever who remained alert, and studied assiduously.

Any leaf in the wind, however, was enough bait to lure him from class. Stan, respectful and courteous, always gave me notice when he planned to throw the hook. He perhaps would notify the Special Services office that he would be absent, but much more often, being on campus, he would come to his classroom where I was awaiting him and sign to me from the door that he wouldn't be attending that day. (*He amazingly always seems to arrive after I did and before the instructor did. His timing was perfectly planned.*)

While I personally believe Stan's absenteeism was irresponsible and undisciplined, I viewed it as none of my business. His attendance record was a matter for his teachers and him to resolve. Once, though, Stan told me he was too tired to go to class and that he was going to breakfast at Carrow's restaurant instead. He invited me to go with him. I was hungry, and I have always enjoyed Stan's company. I had an unexpected hour and a half to spare, but I declined. I believe that my having breakfast with him instead of our attending class would have appeared to support behavior I consider erring and desultory. My decision was admittedly a judgement call. It was made in accordance with the principles expressed in this chapter. Stan's attendance record improved markedly as his college career drew to a finish. (*The year after Stan's graduation, I flew to Pennsylvania to interpret during his wedding. He married a lovely hearing bride. They have since adopted an infant son who is deaf.*)

Samuel The Surreptitious

Deafness came upon Sammy suddenly when he was 14 years old. It was unexpected and unexplainable, or—at least to Sammy—was unexplained to his satisfaction. He acknowledged he would probably always be deaf, but he didn't like it. Sammy's deafness left him with perfectly understandable speech and an attitude that he'd been ripped off. Surprisingly, in spite of feeling resentful and owed, Sammy was cheerful and witty. His sign language skills developed rapidly. He often used ASL cleverly to humor us all.

I served as Sammy's interpreter in a few classes at the college. I grew to like him early on. He never complained about his being deaf, but if I asked him about his deafness, bitterness quickly surfaced. (*Regardless, I opened the topic occasionally because I wanted to examine and learn from his perspective. ALL (!) other deaf people I know have let me know that their deafness was okay with them. For Sammy, deafness was definitely NOT okay.*) In an effort to show kindness, I told him—as I have told some others—that I would be glad to interpret for him should he occasionally need an interpreter off campus.

Later on Sammy asked me if I would accompany him to the Social Security Administration's local office to interpret an interview the SSA wanted to conduct with him. Their procedures to determine Sammy's continued eligibility for receiving SSI benefits (*money*) required a periodic interview and, of course, a pound or two of paperwork. In the car, on the way to the office, Sammy informed me that he would not be using his voice at all and that he would not give any evidence he could lipread. He would wait for me to sign everything spoken and he would sign all of his responses, which I was to voice. He told me he would be "very very deaf."

Sammy's strategic tactic was Machiavellian. He explained to me that the Social Security Administration does not look as favorably on a person with understandable speech as on a person who does not speak. (*If Sammy is right about this, may enlightenment shine upon the interviewers of the deaf in our government.*) My reaction to his instructions was, "Okay, fine." His relationship with the SSA is his business, not mine.

Lois The Incessant

Lois complained. Her complaining was unending and unremitting. Lois raised a fuss about everything except her deafness. She used her deafness as an opener to express her discontent with hearing people. She found fault with the teacher, with his assignments, with his grading, and with the textbook. She was dissatisfied with the lighting in the classroom. She protested about other students in the class when they participated in discussions. She bellyached about the weather, her car, and her dog. Lois was a rapid staccato-signing, gold-medal malcontent.

The deaf person's view of life, bleak or sunny, is not to be an interpreter's concern. But with Lois, all of her negativism was signed to me personally, her interpreter, as an ongoing private monologue. And I do mean ongoing!

Moreover Lois wanted her monologue to become our dialogue. When she was disinterested in the class (*often*), she tried to draw me into a chat mode. She wanted me to listen to her harangue, comment, *AND* interpret all at the same time.

During class breaks Lois pursued me wherever I would go (*except into the men's room, which became my sanctuary*), and her magniloquence unbelievably picked up the pace. (*One evening I phoned her other interpreters to see if they were having the same experience. They were.*)

Once, when the instructor announced a break, I beat feet out the building and sat alone on the campus ground, my back resting against a tree trunk. Soon Lois was standing there with conversational hands flying, soaring above me. I didn't try to follow what she was saying until her hands glided to a stall. Then she signed to me, "Why did you leave the room so fast? Are you okay?"

If Lois had not opened that door of opportunity for me then, I soon would have opened it myself. With a genuine smile on my face, I explained to Lois that class breaks, for me, are breaks from communication, especially sign language communication. "I rest and regain energy best when I am alone and still," I told her. "This class is long and intense. It is somewhat difficult to interpret, and my difficulty is compounded by your signing to me personally during the lecture. I'm going to ask you not to do that anymore. I am, please remember, the teacher's interpreter as much as I am yours. I want to do a good job for him too."

Lois received the content of my message with a smile, but the remaining parts of her facial expression told me the concept of my message evaded her.

Over a short time Lois's talking to me during class stopped. She did, however, struggle unsuccessfully with allowing me solitude during breaks. She adjusted, and I adjusted. Kindness, I realize, sometimes requires a cordial straightforward telling of my needs too, and a willingness to accept the other person's efforts to meet them.

"There can be no transforming of darkness into light and of apathy into movement without emotion."

—Carl Gustav Jung

"The blind eye sees no light and no darkness; the blind eye sees nothing."

—Jim Brewington

Chapter 8

Scruples or Standards?

(Interpreter Ethics)

Ethics is a huge subject. Ethics is a topic discussed by psychotherapists and lawyers, by physicians and clergy, by other professionals, and clients of professionals. Ethics are debated into the wee early hours of dark mornings by students of philosophy. But surely, your nose is not in this book to load up on the latest in philosophical ethical thought.

Sign language interpreters are taught ethics. Perhaps you'd like to know what those ethics are so you'll know what to expect from us. I'd like to give you a simple list of principles. Unfortunately, I have no such list.

Many interpreters belong to a professional organization called The Registry of Interpreters for the Deaf (**RID**). RID is an excellent organization of high standards. It tests and certifies interpreters all of whom are highly skilled. RID interpreters are obligated to abide by the Rid Code of Ethics, which is reproduced verbatim below (*and on the Rid website at www.rid.org*).

Code of Ethics

The Registry of Interpreters for the Deaf, Inc. has set forth the following principles of ethical behavior to protect and guide interpreters and transliterators and hearing and deaf consumers. Underlying these principles is the desire to insure for all the right to communicate.

This Code of Ethics applies to all members of the Registry of Interpreters for the Deaf, Inc. and to all certified non-members.

1. Interpreters/transliterators shall keep all assignment-related information strictly confidential.

2. Interpreters/transliterators shall render the message faithfully, always conveying the content and spirit of the speaker using language most readily understood by the persons(s) whom they serve.

3. Interpreters/transliterators shall not counsel, advise or interject personal opinions.

4. Interpreters/transliterators shall accept assignments using discretion with regard to skill, setting, and the consumers involved.

5. Interpreters/transliterators shall request compensation for services in a professional and judicious manner.

6. Interpreters/transliterators shall function in a manner appropriate to the situation.

7. Interpreters/transliterators shall strive to further knowledge and skills through participation in workshops, professional meetings, interaction with professional colleagues, and reading of current literature in the field.

8. Interpreters/transliterators, by virtue of membership or certification by the RID, Inc., shall strive to maintain high professional standards in compliance with the Code of Ethics.

I admire RID for the work they do, and I admire RID-certified interpreters for the skills they possess. Many proficient, talented interpreters, however, are not RID-certified and don't want to be. Some of my colleagues have told me that they will not submit to the RID Code of Ethics because it is underdeveloped for and inattentive to the educational setting. I agree. I personally do not want to be governed by a code of ethics, because the ethics seem more concerned with good and bad behavior than with moral duty and obligation. Also, as I wrote in Chapter 7, written professional codes of ethics tend to *restrict* what a professional may do while moral correctness tends to *expand* what a professional may do.

I believe that situational morals—morals determined on-the-fly as the circumstances are perceived—are a contrived, groundless, and potentially risky set of guidelines. Conversely, I believe that the idea of situational ethics can be a strongly valid concept for a person to embrace. Situational ethics is a system of ethics that is based on love and by which behaviors are judged within their contexts and not by stated principles or rules. Situational ethics is a good way to go only if the required love is built upon an unchanging moral foundation. I have tried to describe such a moral base in Chapters 6 and 7 wherein I discussed the interpreter-teacher relationship and the interpreter-deaf student relationship.

A professional written code of ethics could, I suppose, make provision for an unconditional moral bedrock that allows for situational ethical decisions, but the wording would have to be so specific and copious that the code would be as cumbersome as the United States Revenue Code. On the other hand, a code of ethics could be written so unspecifically and vaguely that the result, diluted and meaningless, would be no guideline at all. Consequently, I have concluded that my personal moral standard, based on love that includes kindness and service to others (*as defined in previous chapters*), won't allow me to be wedded to a code of ethics.

If I could describe one situation or behavior that would technically violate the Code of Ethics but, which for me, would be morally correct, that would be sufficient reason for me to avoid submitting to that Code of Ethics. Here is a short list of three such situations.

(1) The Code states, "Interpreters/transliterators shall keep all assignment-related information strictly confidential." The Special Services policy at our college requires the interpreters to report deaf students' absences to the office. Additionally, we are supposed to inform our supervisor if we assess the deaf student is not fully benefitting from the interpreter services or if we believe the deaf student is not doing well in the class. We interpreters can't submit to the ethic *and* follow the policy. Because I believe that the policy is designed for the benefit of the student and that obeying the policy doesn't violate the student's privacy, I choose to regard the policy and disregard the ethic.

Would keeping "*all* assignment-related information *strictly* confidential" mean I couldn't tell my wife, Debbie, and our sons, Brent and Chad, where I am going or what I will be doing? That may seem like an absurd and ludicrously literal application of the concept, but I've listened to some of my colleagues seriously discuss and defend such a reading!

The idea of keeping one's mouth shut regarding other peoples' lives and business is generally a good one. Certain professionals such as lawyers, physicians, therapists, and pastors have a confidentiality privilege protected by law. But the law mandates exceptions. (*The clergy-penitent privilege is thankfully still intact.*) I applaud the biblical concept that "a prudent man keeps his knowledge to himself, but the heart of fools blurts out folly." (*Proverbs 12:23*) "A prudent man" and "fools" imply persons who make decisions based on wisdom or lack of wisdom respectively. The Code of Ethics makes provision for neither. For an interpreter who is a front-line member of the educational team, this blanket rule from the Code of Ethics is, in my opinion, unworkable.

(2) The Code states, "Interpreters/transliterators shall not counsel, advise, or interject personal opinions." Perhaps, just maybe, an interpreter could execute this ethic at the postgraduate level, but for the preschool through baccalaureate levels, the tenet is preposterous, irrational, and self-defeating. For deaf students in the very early grades, interpreters teach ASL, help with coats and mittens, accompany to the restroom, and, in many other ways, serve almost as a parent-at-school. In high school and college, deaf students frequently ask their interpreters for opinions and advice on a variety of subjects like which book to read for the report, which project to choose, and who is the best teacher for the next math course. The interpreter's relationship with the deaf student is usually daily, alive, and interactive. (*See Chapter 7 for more detailed information about the interpreter-deaf student relationship.*) Strict adherence to the Code would seriously alter the deaf student-interpreter relationship as it tends to naturally formulate. I believe such alteration would impede the deaf student's educational progress.

(3) The Code states, "Interpreters/transliterators shall request compensation for services in a professional and judicious manner." This seems like a good practice, however hidden in this rubric is a maxim that I have heard presented strongly at interpreters' seminars. I've been informed in no uncertain terms by workshop leaders and some colleagues that interpret-

ers shall request (*require!*) compensation for services no matter what. Working for no charge or a discounted rate, they argue, undermines the market for interpreters who depend on their profession to make a living. I don't buy the argument, but moreover, if I believe that in certain circumstances I should provide my services for no charge, I will do just that. Such a decision is, for me, a moral decision that supersedes a decision based on devised professional ethics.

I have seen deaf people express their approval of RID's certification procedure and requirement that their certified interpreters "shall strive to maintain high professional standards in compliance with the Code of Ethics." Deaf persons know that if a RID-certified interpreter violates their privacy or confidentiality or if the interpreter provides an inadequate service, the deaf have recourse to report the interpreter to RID and perhaps cause the interpreter to be professionally sanctioned. (*I suppose hearing clients have the same recourse.*) RID processes such complaints and appeals through a component of their organization called the Ethical Practices System.

The reality that many deaf clients prefer RID-certified interpreters is understandable. Hopefully I have straightforwardly asserted my belief that no code of ethics that can guide the educational interpreter effectively down the road of right behavior exists. A good law will always be inferior to a loving heart.

One other point of ethical issue concerns me. I would like to direct your focus to a matter that has become a bone of contention for me.

Withdrawing Interpreter Services

Removing interpreter services from certain deaf college students is becoming more and more a popular policy, popular with administrators but not highly touted by students, teachers, and interpreters. The decision to withdraw services is made when the deaf student has, ostensibly, abused the interpreter's services. (*Abusing the interpreter's services is not the same as abusing the interpreter, though the line between the two is thin and pale.*) A deaf student's unexcused absence from class would be considered abusive, for example, especially if the interpreter shows up, sits up, and is ready to start. Unexcused absence is loosely defined, but in general it means that the deaf student didn't notify the college office he isn't coming to class early enough for the office to call the interpreter at home and say, "Don't come in. The student won't be here."

At our college if a student—or teacher—is absent without notice, the interpreter is paid for the obligated time anyway. If the student has three such absences in one semester, his interpreter services may be summarily terminated. To my knowledge a no-notice absence is the only offense that's ever been used to execute the provision of the policy allowing the administrators to jerk the interpreter. (*At our college, the need to enforce the policy is rare indeed. The policy is nevertheless in place and is occasionally invoked.*)

Administrators of interpreter services with whom I work, and others with whom I've spoken, believe the policy to withdraw services is a good one grounded in sound fiscal- and people-management principles. Our college's legal advisors counsel us, so I am told, that withdrawing interpreter services for three absences-without-notice is not a violation of the Americans With Disabilities Act's Equal Access provision, so the policy enjoys solid legal footing.

I, on the other hand, am opposed to the policy and the practice. I believe the policy has no solid footing, fiscal, social, or educational. (*I'm not qualified to have an opinion about a legal footing.*) Moreover, the policy is unethical and immoral.

Below are listed the arguments in favor of the policy as they have been presented to me. Then to rebut those arguments I have expressed my thoughts. Finally, I have listed and enumerated further reasoning that supports my opposition to the policy.

Withdrawing Interpreter Services

IN FAVOR:

THE FISCAL ARGUMENT

Special Services operates on a shoestring. Our budget is tight and strictly controlled. We don't have enough money for the office supplies we need. We can't afford to pay interpreters for students who don't show up. To continue to do so exhibits lousy fiscal responsibility to the taxpayers and other contributors who support the college—and to the students who fork over their tuition money.

REBUTTAL TO:

THE FISCAL ARGUMENT

The exercise of good stewardship and making wise decisions with one's money *is* a good idea. Surely that's axiomatic. Unwise use of money, especially allocated money, does demonstrate irresponsibility to contributors. That too is a given. But good fiscal responsibility involves going after more money if more money is needed. If deans and department heads are discontent with the amount of money budgeted for them, why don't they plead their cases in the faces of the people who determine money allocations? Here, the case we're pleading is for the deaf. Why are services for the disabled operating on a shoestring in California, one of the most affluent political entities on the planet? Why are decisions about interpreter services made on fiscal factors in a country where equal access for the deaf is federally mandated? My guess is that plenty of oil is available for the hinge that squeaks loudly enough. But sometimes squeaky hinges aren't oiled; they're replaced by new ones. Therefore some overseers of interpreter services are shy about squeaking, fearing their creak will grate the senior bosses.

For good or bad, college administrators are political animals—at least in part—whether they like it or not. The political aspect of their jobs suggests that they shouldn't rock any boats.

Money is a tool. Usually professionals are more highly regarded if they use the right tool or the necessary amount of material to complete a job. College administrators, so it seems, believe trying to complete the job with insufficient funds is praiseworthy. I disagree.

Money is a logistical device. Any creative process requires considering the concept before considering the logistics. First, one should define the desired result, then one should figure out how to achieve that goal. If the logistics are reviewed first, the creative process is stifled. The methods, resources, and techniques for accomplishing goals are practically limitless, but the creative ideas—and the unstoppable desire to do the right thing regardless of the consequences—are in short supply.

I learned this important principle from a former employer, a sharp businessman skilled at putting together buy-and-sell business deals. For meetings—when another businessman and he met to create a transaction—he would bring along his attorney and accountant. He had them wait in another room while the two principals met, talked, and designed a deal they both liked. After the deal was formulated, the attorney and accountant were invited in. The concepts of the agreement were given to them. Then the accountant and attorney were told to make it happen and make it legal.

My friend and former employer explained to me, "If you bring in the logistics professionals when you're trying to create, they will sit there and tell you all the reasons you can't do what you want to do. And there will always be people around to tell you there isn't enough money. If Walt had listened to his logistics people instead of his 'imagineers,' there would be no Disneyland."

Supporting a decision to withdraw interpreter services from a deaf student with a budget argument is a classic example of the tail's wagging the dog. This administrative misdirection unduly penalizes the deaf.

IN FAVOR:

THE IRRESPONSIBILITY ARGUMENT

The deaf students who repeatedly miss classes without notice or excuse are irresponsible. They need to learn that their poor choices have consequences. They're in college now. If they don't learn here, they will find a rude awakening in the real world. It's better they understand now to honor their commitments. Their employers won't tolerate no-show behavior. We're really doing these students a favor by making them more responsible. It's part of our job to teach them this important lesson.

REBUTTAL TO:

THE IRRESPONSIBILITY ARGUMENT

My rebuttal to this reasoning has three parts.

(1) No-show, no-notice behavior *is* irresponsible, unheedful, and discourteous. Efforts to change such behavior may well be part of a college's objective or, at least, a desired by-product of a good education (*especially at the college level*). But an interpreter's job does not involve changing the behavior of deaf people. Assigning values to their behavior, moral values, religious, ethical, or cultural values, is not the responsibility of their interpreter or of those who provide interpreter services. Interpreters in colleges are not present to lead the deaf down the path of personal or

professional improvement. (*See Chapter 7 for when doing that might be appropriate at other educational levels.*) Special Services offices exist to provide support and, hopefully, encouragement for students with special needs, not behavior or attitude modification. Arguably, the college's instructors have the responsibility to guide students into successful study methods and critical thinking skills and appropriate behavior choices, but interpreters do not have, nor should we have, that assignment or commission. Conclusively, interpreter services should not be withdrawn to teach the deaf a lesson. Teaching a lesson may be our concern, but it's none of our business.

(2) Even if someone could present a convincing argument that teaching deaf students to become responsible is a role for Special Services, no evidence exists, to my knowledge, that withdrawing interpreter services is an effective way to do that. On the contrary, "That won't work," say my faculty friends in the psychology department. Punishment does not successfully extinguish undesirable behavior, especially in the long run. The more productive method is to positively reinforce the desired behavior. Reward the deaf student for attending class by the presence of an interpreter and a consequential positive experience in the classroom, at least insomuch as the classroom is a positive experience for everyone else. Surely amputating the interpreter from a deaf student will add enormous stress to him and contribute to discouragement in an environment where stress and discouragement already reign in the lives of many.

(3) Concluding that students who are absent from class without notice are irresponsible people needing to

learn a valuable lesson is a fallacy of reasoning. This logic fallacy, called the Fallacy of Denying the Antecedent, takes the following form:

If A then B
Not A
Therefore, not B.

Here's a germane example. If (A) you attend all of your class meetings, then (B) you are a responsible student. You have been absent three times this semester (not A), therefore (not B) you are not a responsible student.

Many deaf students I know are very responsible, dependable people. They hold jobs, and their employment record is enviable. They are punctual for their social appointments. They are sensitive and responsive to the needs of other people. They meet their obligations, both assigned and assumed. They're worthy of high grades for accountability. Assuming that deaf students who sometimes fail to notify the interpreter of their absence from classes are also unstable, floating souls bobbing adrift through life is a serious misreading. Severing deaf people from their interpreter — believing their jeopardous habit requires dire action — is like revoking a person's driver license because they sometimes allow their parking meter to expire. We're swatting at gnats, and we're using a sheet of plywood to do it. Please, let's stop the overkill.

Here is a list of other thoughts to be considered regarding the withdrawing of interpreter services.

(1) *Hearing* students with three or more unexcused absences from class are not directly penalized. Penalizing a deaf student for unexcused absences is unfair.

If an instructor, or a school, has a policy regarding attendance, that policy will probably be equally applied to all class members. To pile further consequences on the deaf is unjust.

(2) A misconception held by many people, including some deaf people, is that the interpreter is present for the deaf. We are present to facilitate communication between the deaf and the hearing. We serve the instructor, the hearing students, *and* the deaf students. When the interpreter is removed from the classroom, his services are withdrawn from everyone in the room. The teacher is deprived of the ability to teach some of the students — the deaf ones. The hearing students are deprived of the input from the deaf, which is often rich and useful. The deaf are deprived of most or all interaction with everyone except each other. The instructor has a reasonable right to believe the interpreter assigned to the class for the semester will be there all semester. But that isn't the case if the services are terminated. And, by the way, if the teachers are responsible for what happens in the classroom, why aren't they consulted before their interpreter is removed? Why don't the teachers have a say-so in the decision? Removing the overhead projector or the VCR from a class because one student had been absent three times would be a laughable absurdity. But to disadvantage an instructor and an entire class of students by eliminating everyone's interpreter is considered by some to be wise and prudent educational management. Well, it seems to me to be an insensitively unfair practice.

(3) When Special Services reneges on the agreement to provide interpreter services, not only is the

professor forsaken and left in the lurches, but, moreover, the contract with the interpreter is breached. We interpreters agree to work in a class for a semester. In so doing we obligate ourselves to that class for the duration of the term. Often that means we have declined jobs that have been offered to us elsewhere. We commit to the college for a semester. Should the college not commit to us as well? Our income is uncertain and precarious anyway. We are subject to the will and whim of the deaf student. In some colleges if the deaf student fails to show up for a class — and the interpreter does arrive for work — the interpreter is not paid for the full shift. If a deaf student drops a class during the semester, we're out of a job for the remainder of that semester. (*Perhaps Special Service departments should rethink these policies too.*) Consequently knowing we could be removed at any moment is the adding of one more uncertainty to the interpreter. The amount and regularity of our income is already on shaky ground. Knowing our jobs can be terminated at any moment through no fault of ours makes finding another place to play ball attractive. The deaf student is at bat, but it's three strikes and the interpreter is out. The deaf student is absent three times and the interpreter gets the axe. Not only is this treatment of the interpreter morally wrong, it may also encourage the moving on of some skilled, valuable interpreters. How much does that cost?

(4) The policy and practice of removing interpreters from classrooms is at cross-purposes to the goals of Special Services departments and the professionals who work in them. Special Services departments exist, ostensibly, to exhort, comfort, edify, and encourage the students they serve. Without exception, every profes-

sional worker in every Special Services office I have met has manifested, directly or indirectly, a heart and concern for students who have special needs. We are the office on campus concerned with nurturing and with understanding special circumstances. To set ourselves up as disciplinarians from the higher echelons is contrary to the hearts and countenances of those of us who have dedicated our professional lives to assisting the disabled. Such internal disharmony results in external disharmony and the sending of mixed signals to the people we serve. Thinking we are teaching responsibility — and saving money to boot — we have replaced compassion with chaos. We should, therefore, continue to provide our services to those needing them without preconditions and without judgments as to who is worthy and who is not worthy to receive them.

I believe that any one of the above rebuttals or any one of the above arguments is sufficient alone to persuade college administrators to get rid of the policy and stop the practice of withdrawing interpreter services from deaf students — and from others — just because a deaf student is absent without notice some specified number of times. I believe the most effective way of teaching responsible behavior is by example. The best way to teach commitment and covenant-keeping to students is by keeping *our* commitments and covenants with them. The best way to teach someone that we are caring and sensitive to needs is by caring for them and responding to their needs no matter what. We can teach a person to endure and go the extra mile by enduring and traveling that extra mile alongside them.

The above is intended to persuade those who don't agree with me to change their minds and behaviors. The following concluding thoughts are an expression of *my* opinions only. They are an explanation of *my* response to the withdrawing of *my* services. They are not a suggestion for anyone else. Whenever my seniors in the Special Services office have informed me that my interpreter services have been withdrawn because a deaf student has had such and such number of absences without notice, I have always told the deaf student and the instructor that I am willing to continue my services anyway on a private contract basis. I have informed Special Services of this practice, and they have approved! (*This, frankly, shocks me. Where is the argument that we withdraw services to teach responsibility? As long as they don't pay me, Special Services gives me a warm blessing to go ahead.*) How much the deaf student and the teacher pay me, if anything, is nobody's business.

Here are my reasons for providing my services without pay from the college. At the beginning of a semester I commit to a deaf student and an instructor to provide interpreter services for the entire semester. This commitment is both professional and personal. Interpreting, for me, is not a job; it is a role. I am an interpreter, and I am one 24 hours of everyday wherever I am. I always retain the ability to interpret. If I can be helpful and serve in that capacity wherever I am, I will do that. Because the commitment is personal—and I take covenants very seriously, whether the other person does or not—I don't abandon a student because he failed to make two or three phone calls or because he became ill during one class and couldn't attend the next one. I have personally decided that I will continue to facilitate communication between the deaf and the hearing whenever and wherever I can, whether I'm paid or not, because I believe to do so is morally right and not to do so is morally wrong.

I furthermore observe the reality that we live in a society with a bail-out mentality. If you don't like your spouse, divorce. If you don't like your job, quit. If you don't like your pastor, change churches. If a sales clerk hurt your feelings, boycott. If your friend acted like a jerk, hang out with someone else. This kind of separate-and-replace behavior creates walls of defense between people. We would be wise to break down the walls, to fix relationships and work things out, to forgive and reconcile. We would do well to embrace and endure together. The walls between the deaf and the hearing are in place. They are strong. They need to be torn down.

In conclusion, we who are professional interpreters should be regarded as ethical. We should be morally upright and law abiding. Confusingly, ethics, morals, laws, policies, religious convictions, cultural norms, and rules for cross-cultural social behavior—and don't forget the ever-changing "political correctness"—do not always mesh with each other; indeed they probably never coincide. Each interpreter must either decide which set of guidelines supersedes the others in any given situation or opt for an eclectic approach. The conclusion must, however, acknowledge the value that we all have an obligation to treat our clients with respect and kindness while providing them with our most capable professional services.

"Light, even though it passes through pollution, is not polluted."

—St. Augustine

"The difficulties you meet will resolve themselves as you advance. Proceed, and light will dawn, and shine with increasing clearness on your path."

—D'Alembert

Chapter 9

Sum It Up; I'm Short on Time

(A Manual for the Classroom Teacher)

If you have one or more deaf students this term and one or more interpreters, please read this chapter. It is written to help by giving a concise presentation of concepts regarding the deaf student and the interpreter. Here you will find some succinct suggestions and guidelines. If followed, they should enhance your deaf student's learning, dispel potential awkwardness for you, and provide a modicum of stress relief for the interpreter. (*All of the opinions and tips offered in this chapter are put forth elsewhere in the text with more detail, explanation, and elaboration.*)

CONCEPTS

Awareness of some concepts related to a deaf student in the classroom will be helpful. I list them here in no particular order of priority.

(1) Interpreters listen to English, interpret the content of the speech, and sign the interpretation to the deaf. This activity, which is a complex cognitive process, creates a lag time. Consequently, the deaf student's participation in class and responses to your questions will lag a few seconds.

(2) The deaf student may not share your culture. Therefore, some of your references, illustrations, anecdotes, and humor may not be fully understood by the deaf. (*The hearing won't understand much of the esoterica of the deaf culture either.*) We interpreters will deal with these problems—almost always successfully.

(3) Interpreters are human beings, not signing machines. We are not infallible nor indefatigable. We make mistakes, and we need breaks.

(4) Interpreters convey voice tone and vocal emphasis by means of signs and facial expression. Thus, some of our movements may seem exaggerated or overly vivid. Don't be alarmed; we are using facial and body expression consistent with your voicing.

(5) The interpreter and the deaf student sometimes interact with (*sign to*) each other for varied and valid reasons. Such interaction may not be part of the interpretation technically, but it is an important part of the communication and the learning process.

(6) Some English word and phrase choices are very difficult to interpret into ASL. A pun is an example.

Some expressions cannot be interpreted from English to ASL or conversely from ASL to English. If there is enough time, the interpreter may explain these constructions and the meaning they are intended to convey to the deaf student.

(7) When deaf students are visually occupied — watching the interpreter, reading, taking a test — that deaf student cannot "listen" to something else at the same time. No one should be expected to focus visually on two different occurrences simultaneously.

(8) For a deaf student, the lecture is in one language, ASL, and the exams are in another, English.

(9) Because a deaf student cannot efficiently take notes *and* watch the interpreter, a note taker or two should be provided. Usually the interpreter assumes the responsibility to set up and instruct the note takers.

(10) The interpreter is responsible for establishing the best interpreting environment possible. To do that we must consider our placement in the room and our mobility — our ability to move about easily — so that we have proximity to lecturers, video tape showings, demonstrations, overheads, and writing boards. The interpreter should work as close to the source language as is practical. If the instructor — or for that matter, another student — moves about while speaking to point to writing on a board or to maps or for some other similar purpose, the interpreter may shadow the speaker. Even the lighting source and the color and design of the clothes interpreters wear come into play when establishing an environment for clear communication.

(11) Many hearing students are intrigued with an interpreter's signing, especially during the first class meeting of the semester. Sometimes instructors are disconcerted because they've lost eye contact with students who are watching the interpreter. These students usually become bored with us after a short time when eyes turn again to the teacher. However, in almost every class, one or two hearing students will watch the interpreter most of the time all semester. One research study I read showed that the hearing students who watch the interpreter do as well or better academically as the students who watch the teacher. (*If a swear word or a sexual concept is expressed in class, all eyes dart to the interpreter!*)

SUGGESTIONS AND GUIDELINES

(1) When speaking with the deaf, speak directly to the deaf person. Do not address the interpreter asking him to tell the deaf person something. The interpreter serves as a conduit of communication, not a messenger.

(2) If you want to know something about the deaf student, ask *him*, not the interpreter.

(3) Try to maintain verbal order in the classroom. If several people speak at the same time, the interpreter must decide whom to interpret. We can interpret only one voice at a time, and we can't do even that if many mouths are creating a din.

(4) Feel free to interact with the interpreter. Allow the interpreter to interact with you. A consultation between the teacher and the interpreter often helps the interpreter ensure he is clearly understanding a concept, a phrase, or even a word. The occasional brief friendly exchange is okay too. Some interpreters are

not comfortable with momentary chitchats while they are working. I usually enjoy them. We are human beings; it's nice to be noticed.

(5) Cooperate with the interpreter. He is trying to fulfill all of his duties including overseeing the interpreting environment.

(6) Do not ask the interpreter to monitor tests or expect the interpreter to report cheating. Do not ask the interpreter to perform tasks or functions outside of his role.

(7) Meet with the interpreter before the first class meeting of the term. Ask each other the questions suggested in Chapter 6.

(8) Educational interpreters are knowledgeable and skilled processionals. Seek our advice and receive our suggestions regarding communicating with the deaf.

(9) Enunciate and articulate clearly. Speak at a normal pace. Form well-structured, grammatically-correct sentences.

(10) Present information visually as much as you can. Use handouts, overheads, computer graphics, board writing, etc.

(11) Feel free to call on your deaf students just as you call on your hearing students.

(12) Follow the guidelines in Chapter 3 when teaching Shakespeare and similar literature.

(13) Avoid sound concepts and other hearing esoterica when illustrating points, in so far as is possible.

(14) Avoid using words like *this, that, over there,* and *all those* when lecturing with visual aids.

(15) Don't talk during exams or times you've asked the students to study something.

(16) During oral presentations that require the students to listen and write at the same time, pace yourself by watching the deaf student's eyes.

(17) Emphasize the significant distinctions of words that are used technically.

(18) When choosing video tapes to show to your class, select closed-captioned versions. The Special Services office can usually assist.

(19) If you cancel a class meeting, notify the Special Services office or the interpreter as far in advance as possible.

(20) When you can find the time, read this book and others that have been written to make clear our understanding of the deaf in our world, in our country, and in our classrooms. Let us both, the deaf and the hearing, strive to heighten our enlightenment of each other and thereby deepen our appreciation for one another. Then the gap, that has separated us for so long, may be lessened by the fluency between our hearts and minds.

"And God said, 'Let there be light,' and there was light. God saw that the light was good, and he separated the light from the darkness."

—The Bible, Genesis 1:4-5

Glossary

Abeé de l'Epée — A neighborhood priest whose involvement with deaf people began when he met and sought to instruct two deaf sisters. He was the first hearing person to go to the deaf community to learn their language, to let deaf people teach him. He founded the first successful school for deaf students in Paris, the National Institute for Deaf-Mutes.

ABI — Auditory Brainstem Implant, a devise, part of which is surgically implanted onto the brainstem itself, to give the sensation of hearing to patients who have suffered the absence of auditory nerves. A small segment of the population suffer from (acoustic) neurofibromatosis type 2 (NF-2), an hereditary disease that causes acoustic tumors (neurofibromas) to grow usually on both hearing nerves (bilaterally). Consequently surgical removal of the tumors causes profound deafness. Robert V. Shannon, Ph.D., of the House Ear Institute in Los Angeles, among others, is working for the continuing refinement of the ABI.

Adventitiously Deaf — Those who were born of normal hearing but whose sense of hearing became non-functional later through accident or illness.

American Manual Alphabet — The 26 letters of the English alphabet produced on one hand with a separate hand shape or position used to represent each letter.

Ameslan — An alternate name for American Sign Language (*ASL*). (*I rarely hear or see this term used.*)

ASL — American Sign Language, it is a language in and of itself with its own alphabet, vocabulary, grammar, syntax, and word order, all different from English. ASL is known also as *Ameslan* or *Sign Language.*

Audiologist — A professional trained to give hearing tests, read audiograms, understand various levels of hearing loss, work with hearing aids, etc.

Bilingual-Bicultural Interpreting — Also known as BiBi interpreting, a relatively new (*and welcomed!*) approach to interpreting between the deaf and hearing, using ASL and English, whereby knowledge not only of both languages is required but also of both cultures. Interpreting becomes more sensitive to the cultural meaning and significance of specific words, idioms, and other expressions of the languages. The method is considered by many to be more communicatively efficient for both clients.

CAD — California Association of the Deaf, this organization promotes civil rights in the deaf community.

Captioning — The audio portion of a television program, video tape, movie, or the like, that has been transcribed into typed dialog that usually appears across the bottom of the screen.

CASE — Conceptually Accurate Signed English, the use of ASL signs in English word order.

Central Hearing Loss — See *Hearing Impairment.*

Classifier — A hand shape or shapes, sometimes combined with movement, that show size, shape and/or movement of objects.

Clerc, Laurent — The first deaf teacher of the deaf in the United States. He was a friend of Thomas Gallaudet. Clerc brought the basics of French Sign Language to the USA.

Closed Caption Decoder — A device that, when attached to a VCR monitor, will allow the display of a written caption on the monitor screen. The video tape must be a captioned tape.

Cochlear Implant — A two-part hearing device, part of which is implanted in the cochlea, the spiral-shaped part of the internal ear that contains auditory nerve endings, and part of which is an external amplifier that transmits sounds to the cochlear area. The device may improve hearing quality.

Cogswell, Alice — A deaf daughter of a Connecticut doctor. In 1817 he requested Thomas Gallaudet to teach Alice English speech. The attempt inspired Gallaudet to pursue the teaching of the deaf.

Conductive Hearing Loss — See *Hearing Impairment.*

Congenitally Deaf — Refers to people born deaf.

CRS — California Relay Service, began in 1983, this 24-hour service provides relay telecommunications between the hearing impaired or the speech impaired and the hearing. Operators relay communications to the hearing by voice and to the hearing impaired by TDD.

CSC—Comprehensive Skills Certificate, granted by RID, this certificate requires transliterating, interpreting, and reverse interpreting (*sign to voice*) skills.

Cued Speech—A system, used to assist lipreading, in which eight hand movements indicate the pronunciation of every syllable being spoken.

Dactology—Sometimes *dactylology*, the technique of communicating by signs made with the fingers as in the manual alphabets. The term is a synonym for *fingerspelling*.

Deaf—Spelled with a capital *D*, refers to those deaf people who communicate via American Sign Language, adhere to the values, beliefs, and practices of the Deaf culture, and who participate in the Deaf community as distinguished from *deaf*, spelled with a lowercase *d*, which refers to deaf people who are not so characterized. (*Please see the Preface for my reasons not to make the distinction in this writing.*)

Deafness (*Anacusia*)—The condition in which the ability to hear is disabled to an extent that precludes the understanding of speech through the ear alone with or without the use of a hearing aid. (*This definition was adopted in 1974 by the* **Conference of Educational Administrators Serving the Deaf.**) This is the traditional term for a severe or complete loss of auditory sensitivity. For adults, it is used only if the hearing loss is 90 dB (*I've seen some resources state 91-93 dB*) or more. For children, the level is often as low as 70 dB for educational purposes.

Directionality—In sign language, the concept of directing the action of verbs from initiator to receiver (*object*) after the nouns and pronouns have been placed in space.

DMC—Dayle McIntosh Center, located in Southern California, an organization providing services, including interpreter services, for the deaf.

Expression—The skill of transmitting thoughts and communication to another by means of ASL or manual communication systems.

Fingerspelled Loan Signs—Fingerspelled words that, through some modification, become signs themselves, e.g., *gas* and *job*.

Fingerspelling—The expressing of English words using the Manual Alphabet, used as a part of sign language for proper nouns and when specific English words must be expressed.

GA or SK—Coded symbols used on a TDD. *GA* means "Go Ahead" or "It is your turn." *SK* stands for "Stop Key" or "Send Kill" and means "I am signing off and saying Good Bye."

Gallaudet University—A credentialed, four-year university with a prep school in Washington, D.C., it accommodates the deaf and hard of hearing. It is often referred to as "the university for the deaf." I. King Jordan, Gallaudet's president, reportedly does not like the phrase.

Gallaudet, Thomas Hopkins—After graduating from Yale in 1805, Gallaudet encountered Alice Cogswell, a deaf girl. He successfully taught her to speak a few words. Alice's father, Dr. Mason Cogswell, persuaded Gallaudet to go to Europe to learn teaching methods for the deaf. An oralist, Gallaudet wanted to learn the Braidwood method (*a combined method of teaching speech with natural gestures*), but instruction was refused. He met Abée Sicard, Massieu, and L. Clerc from whom he tried for two months to learn French Sign Language. Gallaudet and Clerc returned to America together teaching each other their languages. Clerc and Gallaudet became educators of the deaf.

Gestuno—In 1975, the British Deaf Association published a book entitled *Gestuno: International Sign Language of the Deaf* for the World Federation of the Deaf. The book contains photographs of about 1500 signs and represents an attempt at unifying the signed languages.   Gestuno has not been widely accepted because of inherent limitations. The name *Gestuno* is from Italian meaning "the unity of sign languages."

GLAD—Greater Los Angeles Council on Deafness, this organization publishes *The Glad News*, which reports on activities in the deaf community.   Additionally GLAD provides services for the deaf, maintains a bookstore, sells TDD equipment, etc.

Gloss Word—An English word or words used to represent a particular ASL sign. This "name" for the sign attempts to show the most common meaning of that sign.

Hard of Hearing—Hearing disabled to the extent (*usually 35-69 dB*) that understanding speech is often difficult but the understanding of speech through the ear alone, with or without a hearing aid, is not precluded. (*This term is preferred over* **hearing impaired** *by the deaf community.*)

Hearing Ear Dog — A dog trained to respond to sounds and thus serve the deaf. The training program is overseen by the American Humane Association and was started in 1974 in Colorado.

Hearing Impairment — A hearing loss of any degree in one or both ears. The term covers the entire range of auditory impairment including both the deaf and the hard of hearing, who may sometimes understand speech without difficulty.

Hearing impairment (or hearing loss) is generally categorized into four types.

> (1) **Central** — caused by damage to or impairment of the nerves or nuclei of the central nervous system.

> (2) **Conductive** — caused by diseases or obstruction in the outer or middle ear, usually not severe.

> (3) **Mixed** — caused by problem situations in both the outer or middle ear and the inner ear.

> (4) **Sensorineural** — caused by damage to the sensory hair cells or the nerves of the inner ear and can range in severity from mild to profound deafness.

Hearing impairment is defined audiometrically (*and sometimes educationally and culturally*) as follows: (*The numerical values for the seven categories vary from resource to resource.*)

Normal Hearing: – 10 dB to 15 dB

Slight Loss: 16 dB to 25 dB

Mild Loss: 26 dB to 30 dB

(Loss of some sounds)

Moderate Loss: 31 dB to 50 dB

(A loss of enough sounds so to affect a person's ability to understand some speech sounds.)

Moderate–Severe: 51 dB to 70 dB

(Sometimes called Significant Bilateral Loss, loss of hearing in both ears with the better ear having some difficulty hearing and understanding speech.)

Severe Loss: 71 dB to 90 dB

(Many sounds are not heard including most speech sounds.)

Profound Loss: 91 dB or more

(An inability to hear almost all sounds.)

Holcomb, Roy — Father of Total Communication, he was the first supervisor of the deaf program at Madison Elementary School in Santa Ana, California. He was interested in barrier-free communication for deaf education.

Initialization — The practice in ASL of displaying a sign maintaining its proper location and movement, but changing the hand shape to the manual alphabet shape of the letter that begins the most common English gloss word for that sign. This practice is often discouraged by ASL users.

Interpreting — The process of transmitting spoken English into American Sign Language and/or gestures for communication between deaf and hearing people. In general usage the term includes the reverse process as well.

Jordan, I. King — The first deaf (*post-lingually deafened*) president of Gallaudet University. An advocate for the deaf, he coined the motto: "Deaf people can do anything hearing people can do except hear."

Junior NAD — The junior chapter of the National Association for the Deaf, the oldest and largest consumer organization for the deaf in the USA. This organization works on communication skills, legislation, and employment rights, helps obtain driving privileges for the deaf, etc. Junior NAD has chapters in all 50 states.

Lipreading — Also known as *speechreading*, the practice of determining what an oral speaker is saying by observing the mouth, tongue, and lips of the speaker. (*This method of receptive communication is plagued by its own limitations. Many English sounds are either not visible on the lips and, therefore, are almost impossible to discern. An example is the name* **Teddy Kennedy.** *Other English words like* **my, pie,** *and* **by appear the same on the lips.**)

LOVE — Linguistics of Visual English, a manually coded system developed by Wampler in 1972.

Mainstreaming — The practice of placing deaf children in classrooms with hearing children and providing the deaf child with an interpreter. The supposed advantages for the deaf child include the learning of socialization skills and the greater availability of potential relationships. The advantages and disadvantages of the practice are argued.

MCE—Manually Coded English, a general term that refers to any of the artificially developed manual code systems for representing English, used mostly in educational settings.

Mixed Hearing Loss—See *Hearing Impairment*.

Mute—A physiological inability to speak. This term does not apply to deaf people simply because of their deafness. Some deaf people speak and others do not. Those who do not are probably not mute.

NAD—The National Association of the Deaf, currently has listings of well over 175 different Deaf Clubs in the United States. Many of these clubs have been established to serve specific functions or to serve the needs of special subgroups of the deaf community especially with functions that are social, political, religious, or recreational.

Note Taker—A person (*professional or fellow student*) in a classroom who takes notes for deaf students allowing the deaf students to watch the interpreter without distraction.

NTID—The National Technical Institute for the Deaf, was formed by law in 1965 and established on the campus of the Rochester Institute of Technology in Rochester, New York, for the purpose of providing educational training opportunities for deaf students in technological areas.

OC–DEAF—Orange County-Deaf Equal Access Foundation, established as a GLAD outreach, a tax-exempt, nonprofit organization, serves as a link between traditional social service agencies and the hearing-impaired community. Their services include, but are not limited to, interpreter referrals, emergency and out-of-state relay calling, advocacy services regarding employment discrimination, Social Security needs, educational planning, job development, document translation, career counseling, community education, and bookstore services.

Oral Communication—A method whereby speech and lipreading are the only means of communication used for the transmission of thoughts.

Oral Interpreters—Interpreters who silently mouth the speaker's words without signing. Oral interpreters may substitute words easier to lipread for the speaker's words that are more difficult to understand.

Oralism—A system of teaching the deaf to mouth words and make appropriate sounds to speak and communicate without the use of signing. Speechreading is part of the method.

PASL—Pidgin American Sign Language, basically the same as PSE, Pidgin Signed English, but from a deaf perspective PASL is the using of ASL signs in English word order. This method is sometimes used by skilled ASL users when communicating with less skilled, (*and English-speaking*) ASL users.

Phonic Ear—An instructor-to-student fm transmitter-receiver system for use during class lectures. The instructor wears a transmitter with a small microphone that transmits voice to a receiver held by the hearing-impaired student. The student wears a head set to hear the voice transmission.

Postlingual Deafness — The condition of persons whose deafness occurred following the spontaneous acquisition of speech and language.

Prelingual Deafness — The condition of persons whose deafness was present at birth or occurred prior to the development of speech and language.

PSE — Pidgin Sign English, a variety of manual communication in which characteristics of both English and ASL are combined, generally ASL signs used in English word order. (*I do not like this term because of negative connotations associated with pidgin languages—that they are crude and underdeveloped. I prefer the term* **CASE**.)

Psychologically Hearing — This term refers to deaf people who process mental information and respond emotionally as a hearing person would. The sign for this concept is the *hearing person* sign signed at the forehead.

Psychologically Deaf — This term refers to hearing people who process mental information and respond emotionally as a deaf person would. Less frequently, the term applies to a deaf person who identifies with the deaf culture.

Reception — The skill of watching ASL, or other manual communication, and understanding what is being expressed.

Register — The degree of formality or informality of language an interpreter (*or a speaker*) uses to ensure the appropriate relationship between the communicators is acknowledged and to ensure the language is expressed in words or signs that are appropriate to the originator.

Residential School — A school for deaf children whereat the children usually live in dorms on campus. Residential schools are operated by the state in which the schools are located. ASL fluency positively correlates to longtime attendance in residential schools.

Reverse Interpreting — An older, less frequently used term for sign-to-voice interpreting.

RID — Registry of Interpreters for the Deaf, a professional organization that represents interpreters nationwide. RID tests and certifies interpreters, has an established code of ethics for interpreters, nurtures and promotes growth among interpreters, and has established guidelines as to the role and function of interpreters.

Rochester Method — A communication system that utilizes only fingerspelling, speech, and speechreading to express English.

SCRAD — Southern California Recreation Association for the Deaf, sponsors, coordinates, and promotes recreational activities for the deaf in Southern California.

SCRID — Southern California Registry of Interpreters for the Deaf, located in Northridge, California, SCRID provides professional interpreter services from its membership.

SEE I—Seeing Essential English, David Anthony's visual English system. A manually coded system requiring English words that are pronounced the same to have one common sign.

SEE II—Signing Exact English, a manually coded system for English. Originated by Gustason, Pfetzing, and Sawalkow, it tries to achieve a one-to-one correspondence between English words or syllables and a single sign for each word or syllable.

Self-Contained Classroom—An educational setting for deaf children wherein the deaf children remain in one room and receive teaching from one teacher or several teachers who come to the room. No hearing children are present, and all educational activities take place in the one location. Usually the group comprises 12-15 deaf students who are working below their grade level. This practice is the opposite of mainstreaming.

Sensorineural Hearing Loss—See *Hearing Impairment*

Sign Language—Sometimes *Signed Language*, a manual-visual method of communication that involves the use of a bonafide language expressed via manual signs, fingerspelling, and facial and body expressions and that is received visually.

Sign-Supported Speech—A method of communication by which the receiver of the communication depends primarily on speech and speechreading but understanding is aided by the additional use of signs.

Sign to Voice — The process of transmitting American Sign Language or gestured communication into spoken English for communication between hearing and deaf people.

Simultaneous Communication — A method of interpreting by which the speaker or signer expresses without pausing, and the interpreter expresses — with various lag times — without pausing.

TDD — Telephone typewriter, a device that sends and receives typed signals over telephone lines and displays them visually for telephone communication without voice. A TDD must be located at each end of the telephone conversation. *TDD*, a newer term, is synonymous with *TTY*.

Terp — Slang for *interpreter* or *interpret*. Can be used as a noun — e.g.: "The terp will arrive before the class begins," or as a verb — e.g.: "I terped two classes yesterday, and I will terp one today." (*This term is one I coined, but I am probably not the only person who has coined it. It has a positive connotation as does* **Terper**, *a nickname for this terp*.)

Total Communication — The theory of using all methods necessary to communicate with the hearing-impaired including signs, fingerspelling, speech reading, residual aural capabilities, gesturing, and writing.

Transliterating — The act of converting (1) spoken English to Manually Coded English or (2) Manually Coded English to Spoken English or (3) Spoken English to Paraphrased Nonaudible Spoken English.

TTY — Telephone typewriter, a device that sends and receives typed signals over telephone lines and displays them visually for telephone communication without voice, an older term synonymous with TDD.

Use of Space — Refers to the technique of placing referent nouns and pronouns in visually locatable positions; involves also directionality.

WFD — World Federation of the Deaf, a conference of educators of the deaf held in Milan, Italy in 1880, that voted unanimously to abolish the use of sign language in all deaf schools.

WRAD — World Recreation Association of the Deaf, an organization that plans and promotes sports and fellowship events for the deaf.

CPSIA information can be obtained
at www.ICGtesting.com
Printed in the USA
FSHW02n2008170718
50628FS

9 780741 414243